Many define efficiency as the *execution of a task* without mistakes.
She believes she isn't enough because she can't be efficient *in the search for love.*
But is all because the meanings *are reversed.*
Efficiency is the act of completing a task with **minimal mistakes**.
Measuring these minimal mistakes is when a mistake is done *and corrected immediately.*
When a mistake is done and the lessons are *grasped immediately.*
Don't linger *in the debris of a grave mistake*, go outside, look at it from an air view.
So please, help me help you *love yourself* by loving me.
Help me help you *love me* by loving yourself.
Minimizing the mistakes *and efficiently* learning from them.
Help me help you grow *with the power of love*.
Help me help you inspire others walking *a similar path*.
Help me help you make them see the battle scars and the treasures found.
Help me help you find yourself again,
so that you can find me.
So that those mistakes go from 'regret' to 'crucial' for the future of the good life sprinkled with love that
you should be living.

Help me help you find a *love so real* it gives **reasonable reasoning to enduring all the pain you've endured.**
The one that came from you, *the one that came for you.*
Help me *save you.*
Broken hearted and all

5

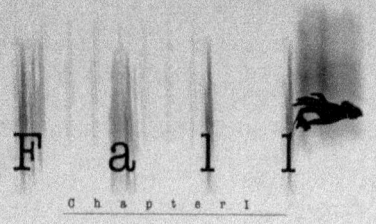

Fall

Chapter1

Hey, I hope your day is treating you
wonderfully. I hope that when you get home
today, or leave it, you get reminded that
life's a beauty.
That *you're* a beauty. No matter how big your
nose is, no matter how far apart your eyes may
be- *you're beautiful anyway.*
The shade of your skin matters not when the
shade of your heart is bright. Trust me there
are people out there that learned to *see
without eyes*, that learned to smell without
using their nose. There are people out there
who *see with their heart,* **people guided by
their hearts.** There are people out there who
learned to *feel first and see later.* People
who learned that the heart doesn't need
glasses. There are hearts out there in need of
hearts like yours. There is love out there,
believe me, I've seen it, *I've lost it.*
There is everything you need out there
coexisting with the things you don't.
Recognizing which is which is the whole trick.
The whole deal. *I promise you.*
Sometimes we get blinded by the pain or the
ego, the pride. The state where your body
accustoms itself to what you've attracted to
the point you believe that is what you
deserve. *That is all you can get.*
And you think you're choosing **the sweetest
devil.** But it's not. Your *worth is set* by
nobody else that isn't you.
Your value can only increase if your heart
really wants it to. **So value up.** Build up your
worth. Look, recognize.
Have pain right there by your side instead of
in front and live. Be free. Be wild.
Be loving.
Be you and I promise you
next time you awake,
the birds will *sing like they used to.*

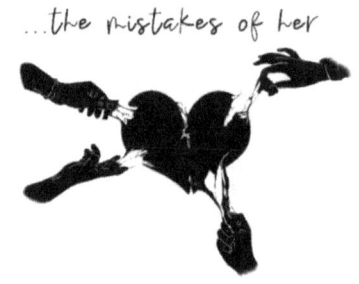

...the mistakes of her

By: Roberto Rodriguez

Love Lesson

She has got *ways of loving* that love had
no business teaching.

Treats are for me

They say *every rose* has its thorns
But she had nuclear codes underneath her petals.
She is safety.
She is danger.
She was *wild and calm* all in a spontaneous
combination.
She was *damnation and salvation all bundled up* in a
package of *deliciously* wild treats.

Changed direction

In *the graveyard of love*. I found your heart.
Dirty, mistreated.

No more.

Constant reminder

Even on the days when the sun *refuses to shine on you* and the moon summons darkness, **you're beautiful anyway**

When the word beauty makes itself *hard to pronounce*.

You're beautiful anyway.

When life does everything in its power to make you look ugly, you're beautiful anyway.

You're beautiful anyway.

You're beautiful anyway.

Deceiving thought

That was the thing about a person *like her*.
She would *flip the table* over
more times than it was possible
and it would **still** *stand*.
She would *crush to fix* and stomp to heal.
That was the thing about a person like her;

She makes death seem *like a good idea*

He won't be there for long

He stood *patiently knocking* on
the front door of love.
Waiting for you *to stop disrespecting its bed*.
Never during, *but after* you did.

You'd open the door and
disrespect it with him.

He will knock again and he will make camp outside
when you seem to have gone deaf.
This is an exhausted man *who knows nothing but*
 the love in the warmth of *your company*.

-Why do you reject him?

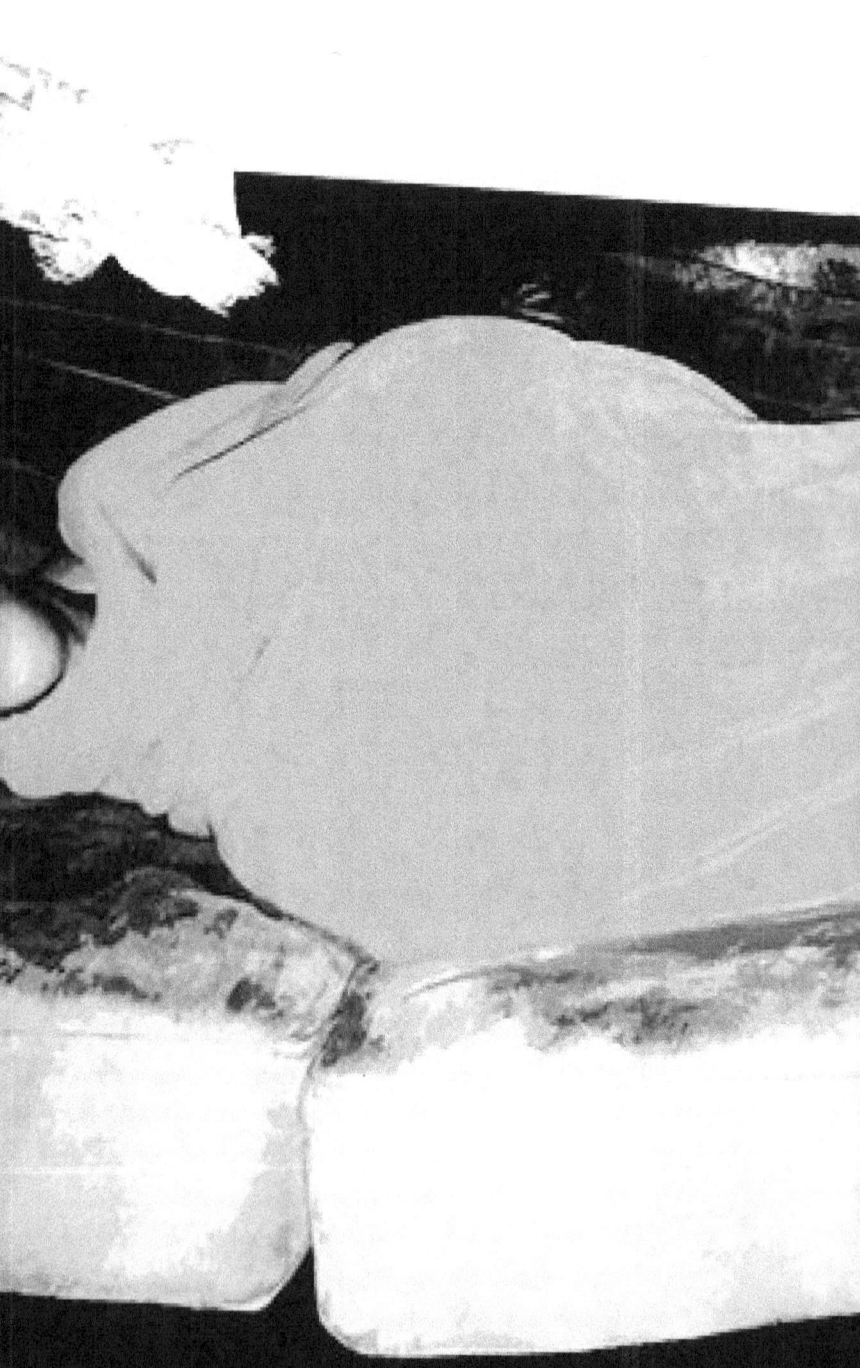

She *loved the poem* but not *the poet*
and i have *always* been *more poetry* than *poet.*

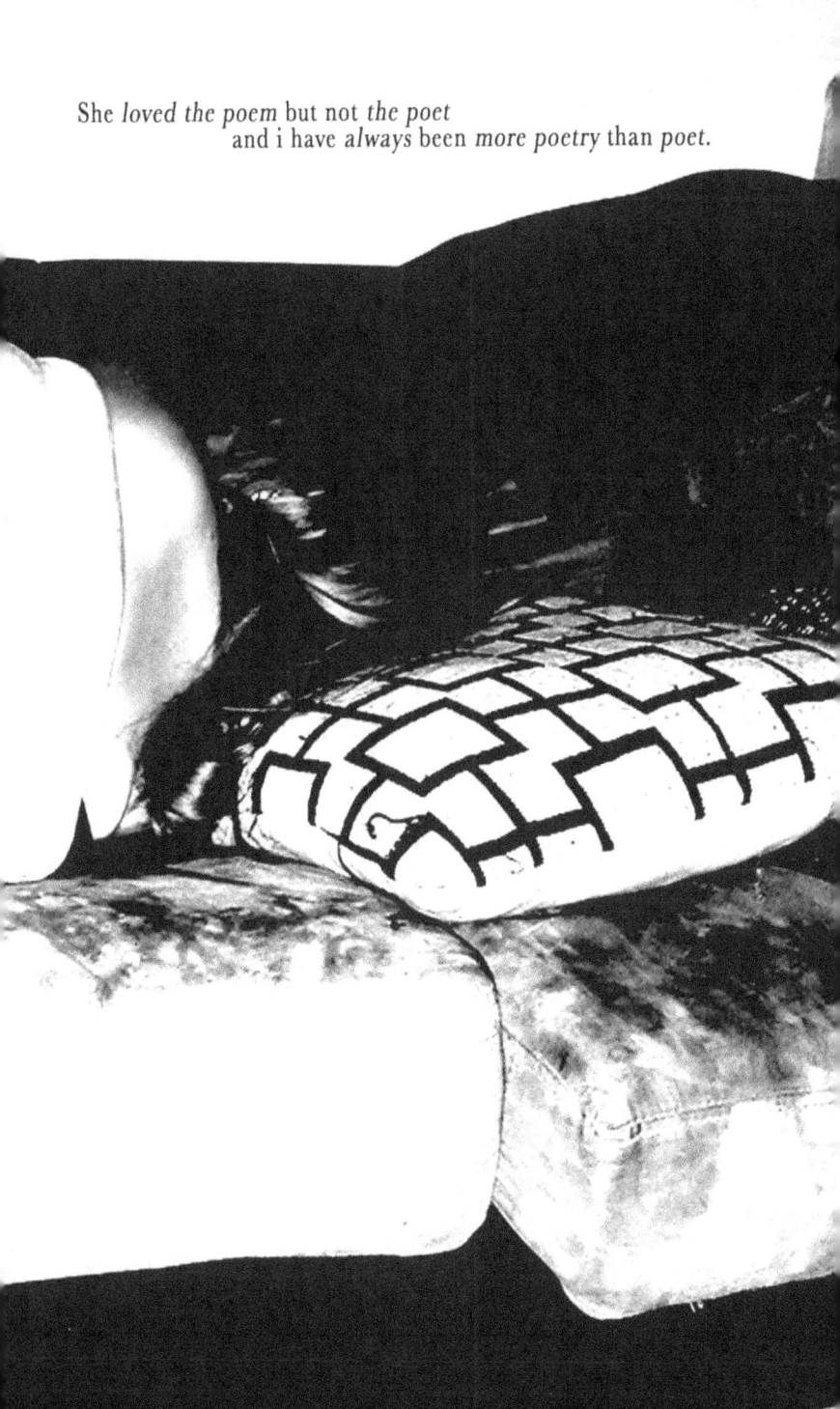

This is why

I'd sacrifice my eyes for you.
I'd give you *my sight* so that you can see you
through me.
So that you can fall in love with you *too.*
So that you can see how you say those *little corny
jokes* with such confidence.
So that you could see the *passion in your eyes* when
you look into me.
So that you can *feel* the passion in your lips.
The passion stuck on your fingertips awaiting my
skin.
I want you *to have* my eyes.
Can't you see it kills me not being able to share a
similarity of perspective with you?
Especially when that perspective happens to be
an *angle of you.*

I want you to *love you* like I love you.

Women Like Her

Women like her are built to be
the *beginning* and *ending* of *men*.
Women like her are meant to be oceans in
a world of swimmers.
Women like her define many who
can't find their own meaning.
Women like her gift meaning *without trying*.
Women like her turn bread into pudding.
Rocks into jelly.
Jelly into rocks.
Women like her, are meant to *cause wreckage*.
Women like her make men like me wonder about
the laws of life
Women like her are meant to
tear *men like us* apart.

The mission

You make my heart *smile* from ear to ear.
My heart doesn't even *have ears*.
It is full of valves, chambers and vessels that all
contribute to the mission of *keeping me alive* for
you.

Do me the favor of *allowing me to do*
one for you.
Don't fall for me.
I won't allow you to listen to love songs at 3:00
a.m., or *resist* a bottle
of whiskey at two.
Our memories won't allow you to *sleep comfortably*
or maintain
a *healthy sleep* schedule.
I will change *the way you look* at others and I will
influence you to *look for me* in them.

I will make you miss me while enjoying my presence.
Miss my voice while listening to it.

Whatever *you decide* to do.
Do not fall for me.

I am not *as easy to forget,* as *I am to remember*.

Don't fall for me because *my*
love will destroy you.
It will leave you begging for moments *you*
neglected.
Don't fall for me.
Because *the strength of the love of me*, is
something you *never felt* before.

New cool

Did *you not* hear?
Broken is the new trend.
Broken is the new fashion.
Keep on wearing their failures *as fragrance*.
Do you not *smell that?*
The scent of lessons *and evolution*.
Buttons of experiences and *zippers*
of harden hearts.

May I just say.
                You *look ravishing tonight*.

Sweet fragile bones

She *wears love* on her skin.
She wears love *on her naked body*.
She wears the fragrance of love even when *it reeks of hate*.
She wears love even when the weather and conditions ask for *a different outfit*.
She wears love on every centimeter of the skin that covers her *sweet fragile bones*.

She wears love **even** and **specially** when she *doesn't have to*.

Mysterious soul

So, the big guy *up there* just made a mystery
and placed us right *in its center,*
and though *I cannot distinguish* which corner is *for salvation.*
I will take *any corner* and *any path* if it places me
in the center of *the mystery that is you.*

Wet grounds

I thought my heart was *invulnerable* to
the thought of you already.
I thought it to *pump blood* instead *of tears.*
and yet here I am,

      still dripping from the wetness of love.

-Wrote this about two weeks after *my son was born*

Ritual of Love

When *energies collide.*
A physical connection joins the fight.
Your body caressing mine, telling me
tales of lies.
Explaining to me the mistreatment you've endured.
The other warmth you've come across.
When energies collide, a physical connection joins
in a *ritual of love.*

Where we sacrifice our *shame* and
excitement **for pleasure.**

I can feel when our energies collide.
How your energy and mine act as layers
on top of one another
and in an attempt *at mockery*, **we do too.**
You feel *every inch* of me and I feel every *measure
of your pleasure*
and like ring to the finger.
I fit perfectly inside of you.

Delish dish

I crave you *more and more every time* I taste you.

Man, how to teach my tongue *to savor more the flavorful* taste of your texture?

Tiny bit

She was a *roller coaster of emotions*.
Ups and downs.
Those downs were only characterized as such because
they *were just*
a tiny bit less good *than*
the usual good of her.

Different *levels of sweetness.*

She was the sugar to the bitter *coffee this world*
proves itself to be.

Mapped intentions

She had a map she *covered up with distrust.*
Every time she told me something different about
her. Her words would *uncover this map.*

Little by little.

Area by area.

Sentence by sentence...
Every time I would **soft: my approach** to **leave a**
lingering impression this map would *show me more,*
it would show me which directions to go
for *a successful love.*
This map she had was imprinted
in her way of life.
It was a map she made subconsciously.
A map **to everything**.

Because the ones without it **found the treasure too**
fast.

Because the ones without it had marked
an x between her thighs.
This map would uncover more every time
 she was *tender instead of difficult.*
It would show me which direction to go when she was
happy instead of angry.
She made this map to trick *cheating souls.*
She made this map to **assure herself of her**
decisions.
She made the map that *lead me straight*
to her heart.

No space

No, my happy place *is not my home* unless you are
there. It isn't my job *unless you go over*.
My happy place is *inside of you*,
sexually and emotionally.

My happy place is wherever
 I am being *cuddled by the love of you*.

Steadfast Love

My love for you *screams in the face of time.*
It demands *respect*.
My love for you whispers in the face of
difficulties.
It demands *perseverance*.

My love for you is to be respected.
My love for you is to be embraced.

"I fell in love with so much potential. Fell in love with an overwhelming amount of possibility. I fantasized about those mornings you never Gave me. I never knew it to be possible, falling in Love with a metaphysical idea of necessity. I fell in Love with the idea Of your Love. Not the one you gave me."

-rob.rod

Longing impression

There is more to her than *what meets the eye*
because **what meets the heart** is always what leaves
a *longing impression.*

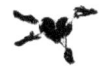

Eye candy

Whenever my eyes start to wander, they tire from
the beauty of the world.
So, they lock again straight on *the*
beauty in your eyes.
Whenever my ears start dancing it isn't long before
music denies the satisfaction only *your voice can*
***give*.**
It isn't long before your voice is the only
instrument *I want to hear.*
Whenever my mouth starts to work out, it isn't long
before I start to crave *the taste of you.*
It isn't long until the flavor of food dulls
because I need
yours *to give me perspective.*

Whenever my eyes *start to wander,*
        it isn't long until they lock onto you.

Second first

Her lips know *ways of kissing*
my lips knew nothing about

-but *you gave* them to another

So good to be..

As soon as you see her face; *a face of simplicity.*

Simplicity in its purest of forms.
Simplicity in *its purest beauty*
and when life passes by, **she simply deals.**

She does what *needs doing so she*
can **return to her smile.**
That smile of *simplicity and peace.*
A smile of bulletproof contentment.
A *glass full type* of smile.
A smile that says a thousand stories *and hides*
millions.
A smile that *feels like home.*

For her, and for me.

They kissed some more

Just one more thing *before you go.*

Can you ask your lips where it was that they discovered that *beauty mark?*

No matter how much I look, *I just can't seem to find it.*

Carefully

Watch out for her.

Not every yes she says *is*
something she should.
Not everything she does is something she should
have.
Just because she agrees *does*
not always make it right.
Just because she consents doesn't
mean *you should.*
If we ourselves *struggle with ourselves.*

She does too.

She battles herself.
If you help, the odds of *two*
against one prevail.
Preserve her *components of identification.*
The ones that caused you to fall.
She is a wild one.
She is a loyal one.

    Watch *out for her.*

Whenever your heart craves for me

If one day you feel alone and I am not
near to grant *you*
the pleasure of my company,
the grace of my love will be
waiting *at your doorstep.*

If ever a day comes *when you feel alone,*

 you can go ahead and **start *dreaming of me*.**

I do not *wear scrubs when* I go to the doctor's
office.
But somehow every time I am going to see you, *I
wear the baggy fabric
of love on my skin.*

Appointment or not

Friends of me

If on the way to my heart *you get lost.*
Just ask for directions.

Simply, ask.

I promise you somewhere inside of me *a part of
myself knows exactly where
it is you need to go.*

Full moon glittered by *the past and thousands of stars* and still, he could not
keep his eyes **off you**.

-but you took yours *off him*

Worlds apart

Our bodies seem to be miles away *from each other*
when really,
they're only a couple of inches.
But you see, if it isn't *pressed on mine*, the
distance even *if in inches;*
  feels worlds apart.

What do you say?
        What do you say **we become one tonight?**

Congratulation

When you forget, *they start remembering.*
When you let go, they start holding on.

Do you really think that's your worth?

Having the need to lose you before realizing
the blessing that you are?
Do you really think *that's your worth?*
Having the need to break you
to *then apologize.*
Your presence is a present.
No one ever received one with a
frown on their face.

A *cause for celebration* is what it is

Servant of Love

Fall in love with a man *who loves you*.
Fall in love with a man who cares for you.

Fall in love with a *servant of love*.

Fall in love with a man who *values you.*
One who respects you.
If you find your instincts to be wrong after
falling.
Gather your pieces.
Get up and jump again.

Nothing shorter than free-fall *makes
this life worth living.*

Before anyone else

What am I to do here with *all this love?*
Where am I supposed to put it?
Who am I supposed to *give it to?*

Yourself, baby.
Give it to you

Right tactic, wrong timing

There are a *million little droplets of rain on her*
umbrella.
There's a couple *more on her feet.*
Some on the fabric of what *she*
covers herself with.
There are millions of droplets of my love
on the surface of *who she is*
and who she is *has her* **standing there.**

Refusing to *let them fall.*

Weakest Liar

You see how those *stories go.*
Girl wakes up after heart transplant, *looks around
and asks* for her boyfriend,
Fiancée, or husband.
The father, mother, or simply just a friend asks
her.
Who do you think gave you the heart?
The girl cries uncontrollably and *a complete sad
story unfolds out of a sacrificed heart.*

I *sacrificed something too.*

I saw you struggle so much it *made me envious.*
Not because I wanted to, but because if you were
happy, I wanted to be too.
If you were sad *the same principals applied.*
I exchanged my pain for yours thinking I'd have to
hold *the weight of mountains.*
I held t*he weight of rocks.*
The best thing I did was exchange this pain,
because now that I feel *what you felt.*
You acted wrong because of your setbacks while I
made sure I acted right while
pushing mine forward.

Mine were heavier.

Your set backs were just ten-pound
weights on my feet.
Mine were anchors attached to my feet and yet I
shifted *to accommodate myself to you.*
I can tell you now.
Your pain was just barely a scratch to *the deep cut
of mine.*
You say this pain held you back from loving me
the way I was meant to be loved.
So, is **'liar'** *really the word you want adjacent to*
'weakest'?

Trust thing

Trust me with **your identity.**
Trust me with your **current condition.**
Trust me with anything that involves trust, *with decisions that involve* **collateral damage.**

Trust me with your heart.
            So that I can *trust you with* **my love.**

Undeveloped characteristics

I'm flawed.
But you see, *I can't admit that you are.*
I don't mean to say that you are perfect because
the definition of that state in society *has
incredible standards.*

But mine, though it is secured by standards of
understanding and compassion,

my definition of that state is you.

Because the flaws you see in yourself *get reflected
as undeveloped characteristics
in my eyes.*
Because your flaws are simple characteristics *a
couple of steps away from qualities.*
So, I will ignore the ones you can't change and I
will help you *better the ones you can.*

I'm flawed.

Your desire to stay now can't be
promised for later.
I cannot account for some things
my hands *decide to do.*
But my heart.
I can adjudge those decisions
to **always be you.**

Seeds of Love

Plant seeds *of yourself in him.*

Every chance you get.

Every *kiss you give.*
Plant seeds of your love in there.
If he *waters his grounds every day*
for the growth of you.

You keep that man.

Allow your love to sprout from
deep within his heart.

They will weep like children

You are the momentum of my blood rushing
through my veins.
The enforcer of **the beat of my heart**.

You are beautiful even *when not appreciated*

Strong when circumstances *label you weak*.

They shouldn't have a say in ***the winds of you***.

They should not have a vote on the aftertaste of
you, and if they think they do.

Simply *blow them away*.

Let them understand the catastrophe
of your *temporary visit*.

Let them sit with regret
on the debris of your loss

Proper burial

I will bury myself *in* **all the good**
that is you.

Fiery sound

So, is today the day you ignite my organs *with the flammable sound of your voice?*

Corresponding companionship

She said she doesn't care about
what she deserves.
She said she only wants *what she desires*. And she
desires your touch.
She needs your warmth.
Even when she deserves someone else's.
She doesn't care about her worth,
why expect life to treat her
fairly when it never did?
Why live a life of corresponding companionship when
you can live a life *of desired relationships?*

**Why *cum all over a man* who earned this, when you
can *cum all over one who never had it?***

She doesn't care about what
she deserves.
She lives life *pleasuring her desires*
and tonight, even though my actions never acquired
enough currency
to *buy her.*

She belongs to *me and my desires.*

Married to chaos

She is not a matrimony girl, *you see.*

She is an adventure girl.

Her heart ventures
places *her mind desires.*
So, when her skin gets used to yours.
When she doesn't know where you
start and where *she ends.*
She will throw you away *like*
a dirty baby wipe.

Her desires change *with the seasons*

Her aspirations *shift with opinions.*
She is not a matrimony girl you see.
The only thing she will ever faithfully marry *is*
the idea that she can get away with whatever her
heart decides to do, simply because *she looks the*
way she looks.

Lemonade stand

Oh, but she will destroy you
in the most *amazing fashion.*
She will **gut your organs and *decorate* them** around
her lemonade stand and she will have you in her
kitchen.

Squeezing lemons for her lemonade.

Wonder girl

She could be *drinking and smoking.*

Dancing and partying.

Her mind could focus on *more than*
a specific thing.
Her mind can juggle a couple of thoughts.
So next time you speak to her and you feel her
wandering across the distance.

She is just **looking at the fire,** wondering about
the cosmos and constellations.

Displayed art

An artist is *she who practices art*
and art how we all *know is subjective.*
So yeah, she's a *walking artist.*
Creating illusions in the mind of the thirsty and
making *bridges that self-destruct.*

She is an artist,
broadcasting *her God given art.*

What to do for an 'out'

Loving you even after was facilitated by the memories I had with you.

Your past **still haunts my future** and *my present seems to be molded by our past*, bettering itself to perhaps **have a future**

The answer

She tired herself from **all the waiting.**
The waiting for *a man to love her.*
She tired herself of the wait and its expensive
demands.

So now instead of looking for a man's love, **she
loves herself.**

Now instead of looking around for compliments, *she
compliments herself.*
She has been training to feel
complete by her lonesome.
So, she completes herself when alone.
She found her own happiness.
She tired herself from the wait and its *expensive
demands*, so now **instead of waiting for a man to
love her.**

She loves herself

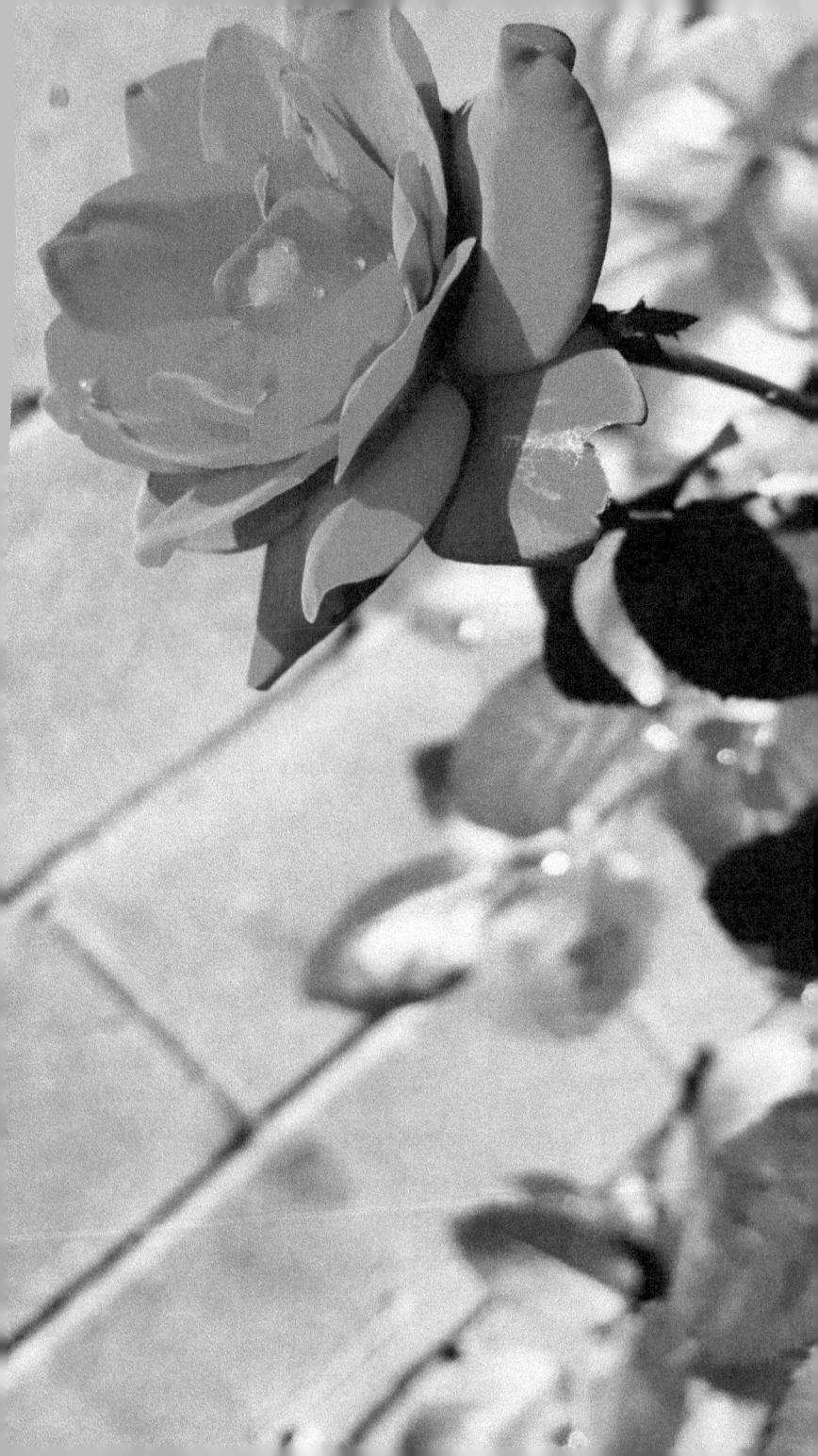

Multiple personas

Tell me, which of the girls who *wears your skin* is
talking to me?
I wouldn't ask but I'd like *to plan* a corresponding
approach.
Is it the one who *hates me?*
The one *fed up* with me?
Oh, *tell me please* is it the one
who still loves me?
I simply need to know who it is
that *I am speaking to.*
Is it the one *that lives instead* of you?
The one who became *because of you?*
Is it the one who **became because of me?**

Please tell me which of *the girls that borrows your
skin* is talking to me, because I am starting to
*believe you are
all of them and a little more.*

...you left him for the other one

He never quite understood *the man he was to himself*, but the man *he was to you* was *everything he ever wanted to be.*

Below within

Oh, *I'm sorry*, I didn't know *it was you* creating
these thoughts in my head.
Didn't know it was you *initiating my desires*.
Simply because you don't like you doesn't mean *I
feel the same.*
Simply because *at times the right words seem to
slip* right through me doesn't mean **my intentions
weren't right**.

I *may be* an oblivious fool.

Foolish *enough to dive* into your waters,
dive into your waters *I shall*
Lacking *knowledge of the creatures lurking
below within you.*

So, since you *subconsciously taught me to love you,
teach me to survive you.*

Bought innocence

So *coincidentally I saw him again*, at the same
time, the same day on the *same bus*.
I would rather say that *than say that*
I planned it.
I would rather say *what I said* than say *I got up an*
hour earlier than I usually do. I rather say it was
accidental than say I *even skipped breakfast*
because I was scared I wouldn't make it to the bus
on time.

I will say that *than say I ran for that bus in*
heels when I've *never run*
for anything in my life.

I rather say *it happened the way I wanted it to*
happen rather than sound like a stalker **or someone**
planning love when love alone does the planning. So
yeah, I'll say it happened accidentally again *if*
somebody asks,
not because I am a stalker but because;

I am *a lost soul* in search of *something,*
anything that resembles the
sound of his voice.

-Straight from the pages of one of my novels

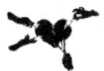

...but she just wants to get lost in the fire to
find herself with me

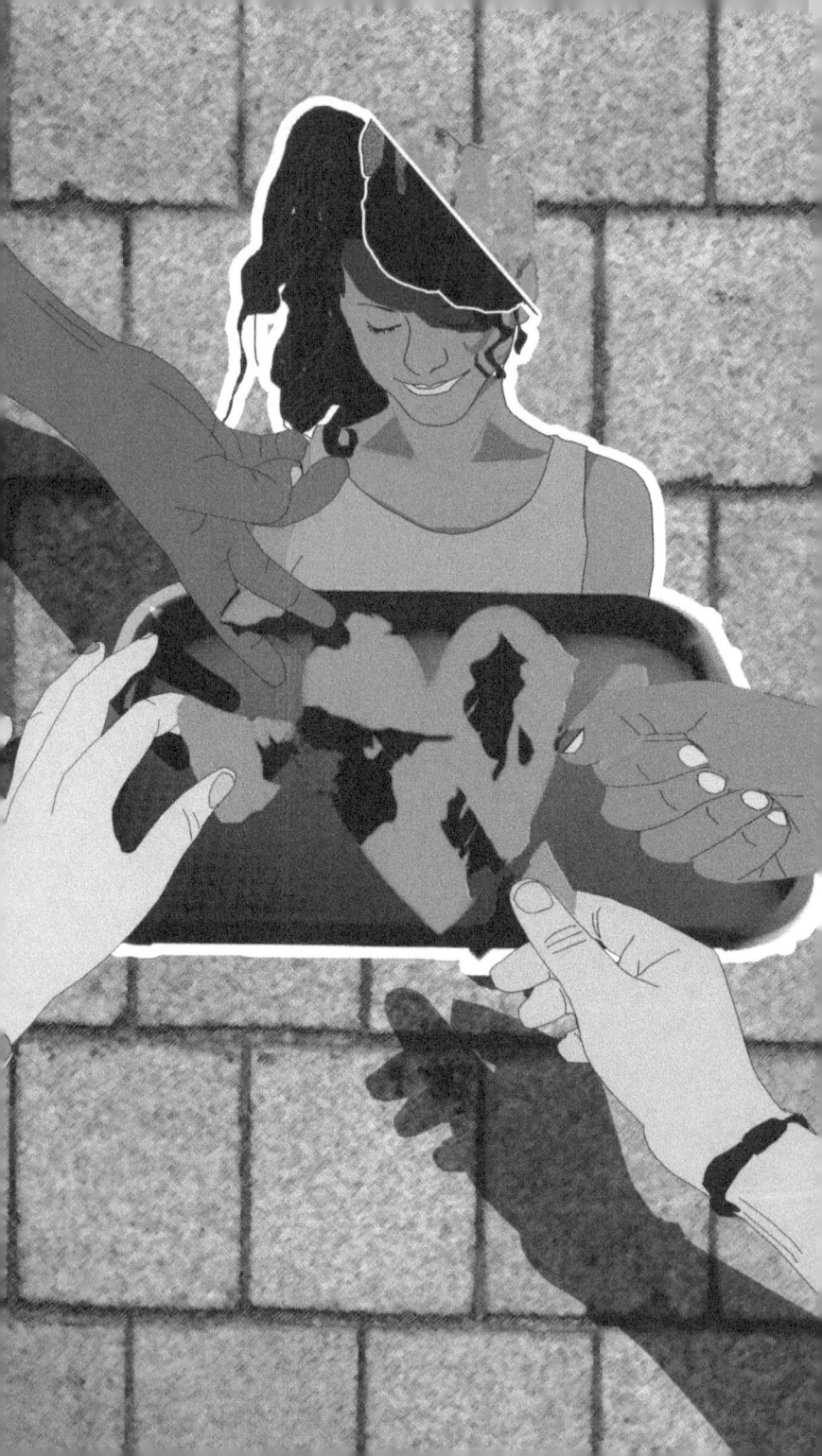

Love representative

My mother once told me that *I fall in love* too
often. Not quickly, **often.**
The expression on her face and *the sounds lurking
in her voice* pronounced these words *as something
that was bad.*

Bad *how?*

Is focusing more on the *beautiful things of her
persona* rather than never looking past her defects
a bad thing?

So what if there is beauty *within everyone?*
So what *if this beauty is only visible to my
evolved eyes?* So what if *I want to?*
So what if *I do?*

Potential should *never be ignored* for it is change
looking for *a reason to happen.*

So what if *that reason is me?*

The perfect girl will never be found
She has *dispersed herself limb by limb in the
bodies of all of them;* they all carry something she
once did.
Fragments of the perfect personality *for each of us
inside each of them.*

So what if you *can't see it?*
So what if I do?
So what if *all I am is the pursuer of company?*
So what if my definition to the blind is
a representative of love? So what if I am just a
simple *sucker for beauty?* My mother once told me
that I fall in love too often.

So what if *I do?*

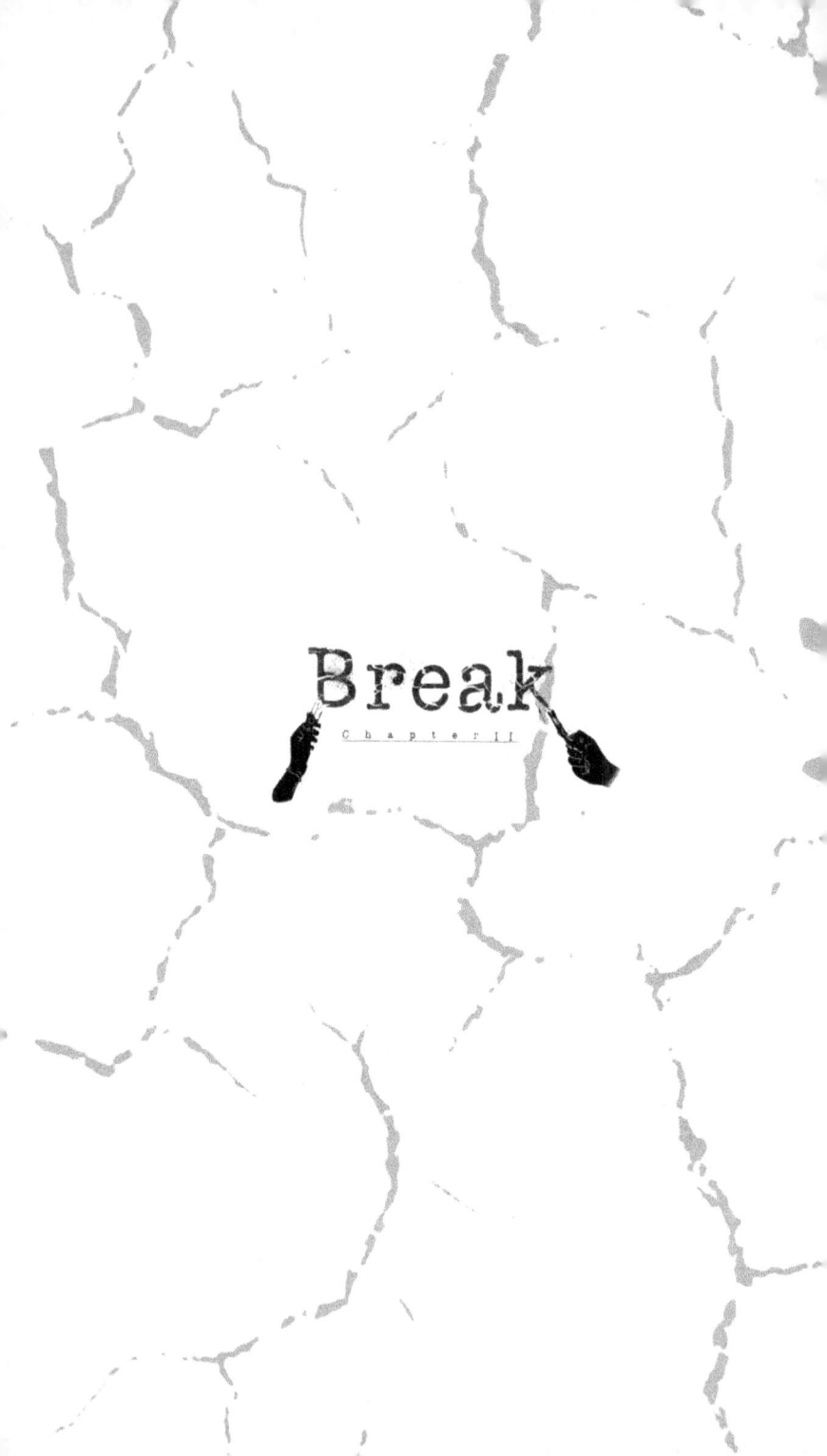

Break

Chapter II

Hey there, I hope your day today is *as beautiful* as
you are.
I hope that if you have an opportunity to
Be kind today, **you take it.**
I hope you realize how much *stronger your kindness*
is over your hate
or even *your ignorance.*

I hope you realize that though you can't go to
Australia and contribute to the mission *of saving
the world*, you *can save someone else's.*
You can donate, you *can try.*

A day at a time.
You can still say something,
you can *still care*

Your heart has *the power* to change hearts.

So please, *love vigorously.*
Hate only actions and negative situations, *never
people*. Never them, *never me.*
Most importantly, *never you.*
So walk on *the path of self-improvement*, prove
your love to yourself and *never set limits* to the
places *you can* reach.

No matter how many distractions,
no matter *how much heartache.*

Be *wildly* free
Be *freely* wild
Be *loving*
Be you

I promise you the next time your heart falls,
love will flow like it used to.

Given all

She believes moments *she wasn't supposed to.*
Built blueprints she *should have* ignored.
She built a home next to a fire, and when her home
was burning down.

She possessed *too little of herself to extinguish
the flames.*

Ambitious metaphor

Want to hear *a joke?*
But that's the thing about jokes-sometimes *the
message gets lost* in translation of laughter.

Sometimes it doesn't have a message to begin with,
simple words combined for *a hilarious result.*
I am getting a bit *off topic* here, want to hear the
joke?
Your heart and his go into a bar.
No

**It was a boxing match and *his heart was already a
professional boxer.***

No, that *was not it.*
The joke was a bit more real than an *ambitious
metaphor*
The joke was supposed to inflict the need of change
and realization.
It was supposed to make you see *what you can't.*
Ready to *hear it?*
Real one this time?
The joke was,
your relationship with *he who undervalues you.*

Yeah I know, wasn't as funny as the anticipation
deemed it to be.
and yet somehow, *look at him*
rolling on the floor.

Look at him dying of laughter.

Best at it

They say *get better*.
Cleanse *your heart*.

How can I, when it isn't even *nearby?*
It is right there in your front porch.

Knocking.
Begging.

Making a fool of itself **once again.**

*Not whom you find it's
where you're looking*

Men *are animals.*

Without a doubt, but what?

You *go to the zoo expecting to see astronauts?*

Ironia

How can you come *demanding the parts of me*
You helped me bury?

-You still dug them out; *you still*
gave them to him.

Partners in crime

You *armed the bomb*.

After your mind caught up to

the *horrors of your actions*.

Your conscience refused to *accept fault*.

Who am I to pay for the *weakness of your mind?*

**Your conscience knew that
guilt would overwhelm you**.

So, it brought *me to the equation*.

Partners of a crime was your escape.

The perfect duo, *victim and offender*.

Who am I to pay for the weakness of your actions?

 Who am I to be put on *trial for your crimes?*

Half human

My only mistake was being **too human.**
Yours was *not being enough.*
I cared so much for so long; you cared so little
for such a short while.
Yet even a microscopic trace of your love *elevates
me mountains high.*
If such little of your love feels this good...
how will all of it?
How do I get all of it?
Because *I help, I look out.*
I do everything in my power to make you notice that
in this world *not one soul* **will ever love you like
I love you.**

Not one soul will cherish you *like I do.*

Not one soul is *hungrier for your presence than
mine.* I crave for you so much my stomach roars at
the sight of you leaving.
Yet you say I messed up.
You say I *brought about the death of us.*
But how did I? When the man I was, was *a man to be
put on a pedestal?*
I was the man those movies *love to talk about.*
That was the man I was but that was
not the love I received.
Yet I continued and I *cannot think of a time where
I won't.* My love for you pushes away any deserved
love *my actions earn;* it forgets about my worth *all
for the good of yours.*
I guess that is where I failed.
My only mistake was being *too human.*
Yours was not *being enough.*

Bear trap

Don't *fall in love* with her.

Women like her tend to confuse
desire with *necessity.*
Women like her *are used to* falling
in and out love.

Do not fall for her, *I tell you.*
She will make you question the purpose of
activities you used to enjoy because you
used to enjoy them with her.
She will make you *see the world* for what it is and
keep *that filter she loves to share.*

So, *don't you dare* fall for her.
Women like her are incapable of loving
people who aren't them.
They are incapable of looking past their
commodities.
Don't fall for her; you see, I too made that
mistake.

Here my leg is bleeding, *stuck on* this **bear trap of
a woman,** and the only worry in my head *is if she'll
ever love me back.*

Crippled *and all*

Fool's errand

If heaven was hidden *right there between* your
thighs, if it was right there *in your chest* between
your arms.

Why *deny me of it* when I went
through hell for it?
When **I first had to nurse your
wounds to lie on them.**

To *kiss them*.

When I had to declaw your fangs so I could *lay my
face* on them for comfort.

How can you say no after *I said yes
so many times?*
If heaven was right there, *hidden deep within your
chest,* how can you reach into mine to *make me
nothing?*
To make **my *ambition toward love*
a fool's errand.**

To make my *pursuit of it* mean nothing more than
another *shattered heart*.

Love therapy

Well you see I *use love as a* **defense mechanism**,

so, *don't you blame* me for loving you *way before* loving me.

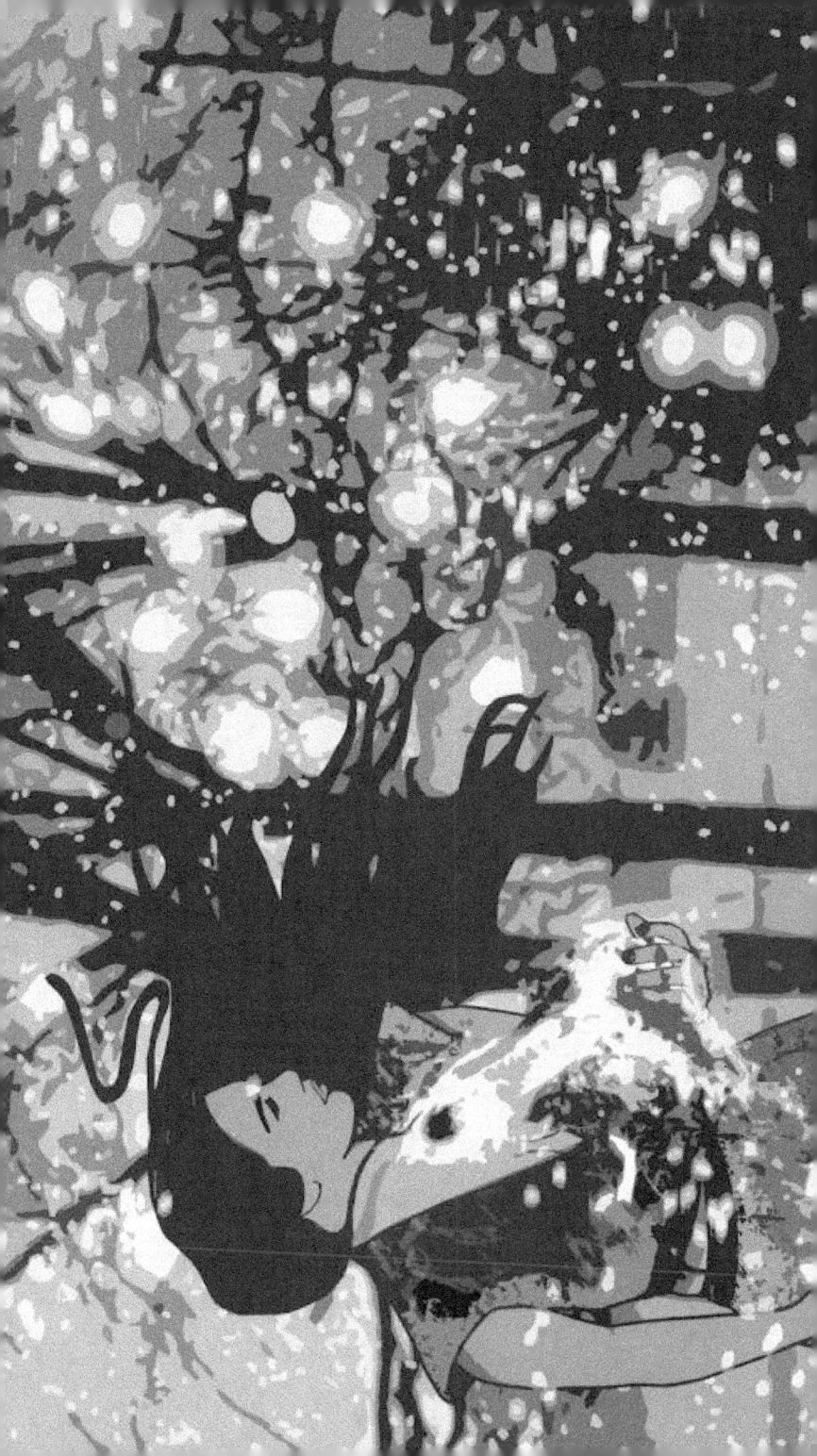

Dead hope

We *hope*

We expect.

Those expectations become *guilty for our imminent transformation.*

Here you go, blaming yourself.

It isn't about *you* or what *you did.*

It's about *me* and *what* I thought *you wouldn't do.*

Emotional abuse

It's abuse too. It is.
Seeing her struggle with what she wants because you
don't want it as much as she does.
It is abuse too. Telling a woman she is everything
every man desires to keep her around because she is
good for your ego. Its abuse to convince her to
stay when *you never intended to,* seeing how much
your deceived emotions hurt her and continuing to
tread on the same path. Its abuse to hurt her *then
allow her to come back for more.*
Its abuse to hurt her and call it love.
Its abuse to confuse her at the expense of
exchanging her happiness for yours.
**Its abuse to call her beautiful and
not call her back.**
Its abuse to answer when you want while
she answers when you call. Its abuse to see her
struggling with the truth of your commitment issues
and allowing her to wait for something that will
never happen. Simply because you love her touch.
Simply because you love the way she makes you feel.
Its abuse to claim love where only lust resides.
Its abuse to *bruise her heart. Is that what we're
here for?* To want what we can't have and ignore
what wants us? To *not want what we can have* and
kill ourselves for *the things we can't.*
*Its abuse to do her the way you have. Its abuse to
treat her the way you do.* Telling her those sweet
words for a specific *sexual purpose.* Telling her
those sweet words for a goal that isn't to *lift her
spirits up*
and when accomplished *exchanging sweet for sour.* It
is emotional abuse to hurt her where
it hurts the most. To *kill her* spirit
for the sake of fulfilling yours.

Stolen Crime

I've *been blaming you* for stabbing me in the back,
Imagining *the bloody intentions* in your head and
the *dirty knife in your hand*
Maybe because I only felt it
and did not see it.
Perhaps because you were right
behind me when I felt it.

But I was wrong, *oh so wrong*.
You *did not stab* me in the back.
I myself found a way to **break my own back,** while
maintaining my position.
While my feet pointed forward,
my hands *looked for a knife.*
While my intentions pointed towards
righteousness, my hands went
behind my broken spine.

I stabbed myself just so *I wouldn't have to blame
you...*

Self-Imprisoned

I understand I am situated *in the wrong cell*
Instead of being locked *away in a cage of integrity
and love.*

I am locked away in this
thick stubborn head of mine.

I know, bear with me.
Only until I am done with my escape

Gifted Soul

If *all the love* this heart wants to give makes
you *go mad.*   Then **break it**

If *all the emotions* that my presence summons
in you *drains you.*   Then **end it.'**

If *my life commitment to the love* of you *is too
big a* responsibility for you to hold.
                              Then **let go.**

I've now *given it to you.*
Have *mercy on my soul.*

Love wrong

Love *wanted me to* be with her.
It wanted me to pleasure myself under her body,
and I did.

But sometimes, **only sometimes.**
We *have got to look after ourselves.*

Even love can forget about the necessities of
your heart **for the needs of hers.**

One more

I am drowning *in attraction* and *promises*.
I am swimming as fast *as these imperfect
hands* allow me to.
I am holding my breath for as long *as
my lungs allow me to.*
I am drowning in expectations my hobbies
keep me from reaching.
Drowning in *an ocean of your
respect and your love.*
If I do not make it to shore this time **like
those other failed attempts**

I'm okay with being a cold floating corpse
in the waters of you.

Destructive favor

No, I *never* did.
I simply roamed around your wreckage.
When you got *used to it* and liked the company of
me *around the debris of your destruction.*
Without cleaning up the mess, *I left.*
I know it hurt, but you can't say I was the one
who destroyed you…

*Someone had already done that **for me.***

Desperate times

Go look for yourself in places you
shouldn't be.
You just might be there

Lost Love

I thought it to be a relationship so
I did not *dress appropriately*.
Denying facts that withstood
my refusal of belief.
Remembering happiness to only remind myself of
the emptiness *and that warm, temporary feeling*.
Instead of solidifying this beautiful
partnership *that could have been*.

We *were* melting the truth *of its death*.

Watering it down so it's easier to swallow.
We were mourning a lost love **we thought
we were cherishing**.
If I had known this to be a funeral,
I would have dressed accordingly.
If I had known this to be a funeral,

I would have acted accordingly.

Dry snack

If *not putting a label on it*

helps you swallow it.

I **refuse** to *be your dry sack.*

Anger overload

You see that?
When your body gets filled with rage your words
get filled with hate.
As if those things *were true.*
You say those things you consciously know
to be a lie *so well*
Her words are so convincing.
She can convince you not to eat *when hungry*.
Not to laugh even when *your humor commands you
to.* Her words get filled with hate and smell
like persuasion.

*So how can I not believe the things you,
yourself say?*

Apology accepted

You apologized for *the general result* of your
actions. You see, **the specifics**
are what crumbled my heart.
You apologized for *hurting m*e and not *for the*
way you hurt me.
You apologized for having me eat your food, when
the apology should have been placed for
cooking it *the way you did.*
For butchering it.

You apologized for the *general wreckage of your*
actions when I wanted explanation
for *the specifics.*
The ones leaving me with **thoughts that hurt.**

'Was this really *who she was?'*
'I am so foolish for falling for *the person I*
thought you were'
'What *does this say about me?'*

Your apologies even when placed where they
should have *been will not be accepted.*
The fact that you apologize for *what it is that*
I feel instead of what it is that you did, *shows*
too much.
It really shows the origin of your apologies
It really shows the *limits of your*
understanding.

Lazy demolisher

Say you *cut your finger*.

You don't amputate it; **you don't cut it off**
for *a paper cut* or even *a kitchen accident*.
You clean it with alcohol; you put a Band-Aid on
it. *You didn't.*

I should have known when 10 was a number
your fingers could not count to.
They can't reach that number
without repetition.

Is it the glue that *makes it almost*
part of your skin?
Is it because *removing it hurts?*

Man, you must really *hate Band-Aids.*

Without Permission

So, what *excuse* do I use?
How do *I explain your departure*?
How can I justify your wrongs when there is
nothing just about them?
What can I say to make it okay?
To make it *not hate me*?

To keep it beating?

Because it *constantly reminds me of you,* it
keeps asking where it is that you are,
it has not seen you.
I am running out of excuses to use,
it asks *me about your whereabouts.*
It asks about your condition when clearly
you don't care about mine.

Do I tell it you *just left without permission?*
What do I tell my heart *now that you are gone?*

In the wildest ones

No.
I refuse *to give it to you.*
I refuse to give you one last time something
you need that I have.
I refuse to give you any more body parts.
I refuse to *stack up the pile like I've been
doing.* Covering them with your dirty clothes as
if blocking the vision
blocks the smell.

I refuse to *hinder my soul* for your presence.
No
I refuse to give it to you.

My apologies can only be in your dreams.

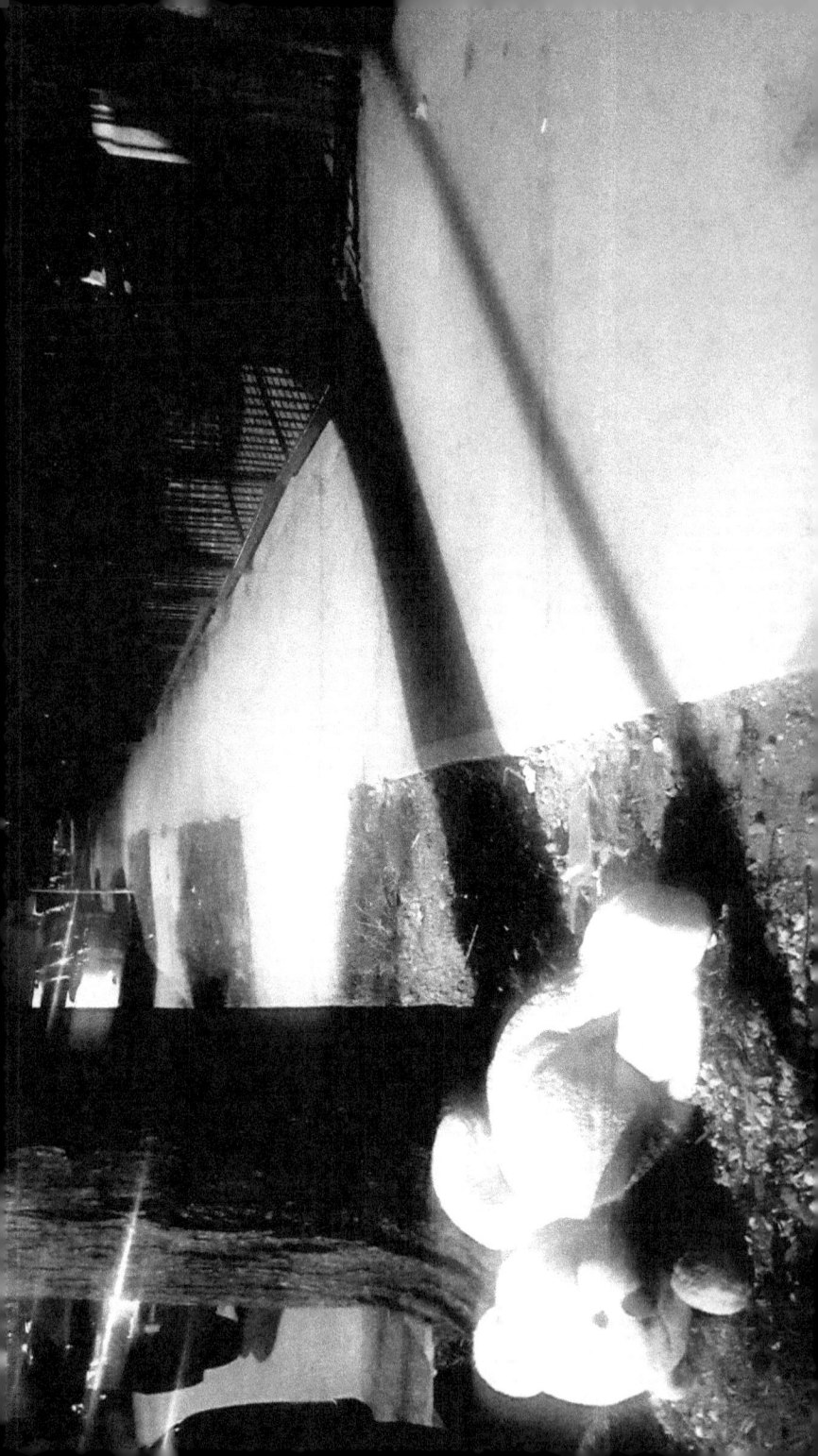

Salesman

What you fail to understand is that he *is a*
sales person.
A direct marketer.
Knocking on doors and *selling to*
whoever will pay.

Selling conditions of his love
that aren't accurate.

Selling warranties of a *reserved pain that would*
Never hold its agreement.
Selling a product that looks like truth and
works like lies.
He is a sales man *you see.*
He will say whatever words he needs to, to make
you believe what he desperately *wants to*
believe. Selling repeated words and *overused*
promises. What you fail to understand is, he is
a sales man.

He knocked on your door *to sell you his heart.*
He conned you and sold you his lung.
You got a fair price though,
given that his heart was *on sale and all.*

Rare find

I have *loved and hurt*.
My heart *has been toyed with just like yours*.
Not like the lost who claim to *feel*
it like we do.
Those who can't see the faces of pain because
they can't look at it from up close.

My heart has been smashed to juiceless.

It has been dry like this world makes *you want*
to be. I have felt
the wrath of the way of the world.
I have followed *the rules it wants me to follow*.
In this scenario,
I am a victim of myself.
I understand that.
But how can I ever make you understand it, *when*
*you simply visited love and I **killed for it?** I*
guess what I am trying to say is.

The excitement to find *you was what made*
me have nothing of value
for you when I found you.

The wonders

I searched the hallways of love for a person *to
lie next to me*
*A person I can look into when I open
my eyes in the mornings.*
*A person I can look at before closing my eyes at
night. Another container because I am just so*
full**, nothing else fits without spillage.**

*I looked for another heart to share my pain.
Another heart to remind mine to pump blood.
I searched the hallways of love for a
person to lie next to me.*

*I found someone who **lied to me** instead.*

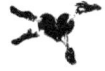

You live in your own skin like *you've never
been there before.*
You live in your own skin *like a stranger.*
Like someone that's *lost their way.*
You live life scared of what your skin is
capable of.
Surprised at the strength
you summoned to move on.
You live like you don't know you,
and that is a tragedy.

Because those who don't know,
desperately desire knowledge.

**So, you wait for someone to tell you who
you're supposed to be.**

Confused blame

She *blamed the world for losing me.*
She blamed the stars, people who *had nothing to
do with our affairs.*

She blamed everything that *ever existed for
losing me.*

Saw it as a sign from the universe *that this was
a false enhancement,* because the blame *was never
hers.* She blamed people who weren't *even near
the fault.*

**She blamed me when I was more
effect rather than cause.**

She blamed everyone and their mothers *for losing
me.*

Everyone but herself.

-She *wanted that* to be my doing

Pain goggles

My heart broke and your love had *no intention of fixing it.*
Even when you had the necessary Band-Aids.
Even when you had the necessary glue.
Simply because you thought your pain to be
Permanent and mine a game.

My heart broke and all you saw were the cracks of your own, **as if mine were temporary.**

Con el guebo limpio

She tried to make him stay *by offering her body*.
He always stayed for a little while, however
long *it took her to empty him*.
Slow strokes to make it last longer.
To make this man fall in love with her heart
and *not her mouth*.

To want to be beside her warmth *and*
not just inside it.

She gave her pussy in an attempt to gain a
little power. But somehow,
 he **left every time he came**.

Peptobismol

So, I am pretty much going to word the conversations
of my actions.
Your time here expired.
So, to the garbage you go.

Your taste is not *worth the stomach ache*

Weapon

Only difference between *that knife on your kitchen counter and those words pronounced with anger.*
Is, **your words don't draw blood.**
They don't leave me *visually bleeding like the knife would.*

You should have used that.
Physical cuts I'll take over the damage of that **weapon of voice.**

Drowning in blood I'll take,
over drowning in my doubts and failures.

Your legs tremble at the *first sight of*

an entrance.

Your fingers tense up, your eyes *wander up*
to **see the pleasure.**
Your legs trembled when I slid in.
Your legs tremble at the first sight of an
entrance.

Your heart doesn't.

I'll carry it for you

So how about you leave the suffering
to the lost ones?
To the ones *too stubborn to learn.*
You have suffered more than you need to
waiting for him to change.
When something grants you satisfaction, you
don't exchange it for something *that may not.*
His ways *fill him with satisfaction,* why will he
change if he is content with *the work of his
hands?*

**So how about you leave the suffering to those
involuntarily detached from happiness?**

To those who have been *taken from* and *never
given to.*
Leave all that extra suffering to the ones
with insufficient happiness.
Let them deal with it.
Because you have dealt *with enough.*
So how about you leave all the suffering to the
ones *stuck on reality?*
Leave that suffering to the ones *buried in
disappointments.*

**So how about
you leave all that suffering *to me*?**

Left turn

You were right here a *few decisions ago.*
Is this how it happens?
1, 2, 3 gone?
Is that how fast time goes?
What happens to the *halves and quarters?*
Whatever happened to the *little traces of
doubts*?
The almost that *almost became?*
What about what became and almost changed?
What happens to *me if I choose wrong?*
What happens to me if *I can't go back?*
You see *people allow themselves honest mistakes*
and when what always happens, happens, they
blame everything *but
their own stupidity.*
Because what right do you have
to a second chance?
what right do you have to expect better
treatment *than the one you give?*

**You think its fine to *treat me like shit and
expect high maintenance treatment?***

Decisions are like seconds, *there is no way to
turn those back.*

Expected hold

He *made you promises* to **break them**

Yet here you are, *crying for him*

Begging him to take you back.

For what?

So he *can keep doing to you* what *he is constantly doing to those promises?*

Questionable answers

I could not *find a way to live.*
But I found you, within you, the 'us' we became.
You taught me.
I finally learned how to answer obvious
questions and *ignore*
the complicated ones.
I learned what path to take for *faster travel.*
I learned all the things you had to, *from you.*
But the life I *learned to live was not mine.*
I should have known that to know the fastest
routes, *I had to time and travel through the*
slow ones.

My presence had to be present for knowledge
accommodated to my perspective.

I should have known the things you *accustomed*
yourself to were a size a bit too small for
these **obese desires of mine.**
I should have known your *reserved necessity*
would accept any words that resembled an answer
to those complicated questions.
I should have known that *those stolen answers*
could only invite more questions.

But I know now.

Now the damage a deceived lifestyle did
attacks the one I lived.
Now those answers *morphed into my own*.
I am not one for insecurities, but here I am
 questioning answers that do their job.

Atrocious Heartbreak

I really do believe we were meant *to build
something so dangerous* it resembled *an atrocious
heartbreak.*

*We had the ingredients and the recipe.
The laughs, the connection,
 and the personality.*

-but you left me for that other guy

Funny thing

I lay my *skeletons on the sheets of your bed.*
I undressed myself to you and for you *even in*
your kitchen.
Trying to peek into the cabinets.

Hoping *we accidentally open one.*

I gave myself to you willingly *out of pure*
desire.
I gifted you parts of myself **wrapped as**
Christmas presents.

You threw at me pieces of a puzzle
I had *no interest in solving.*

Funny thing *is I actually tried to.*

Damaged goods

Your own failures and fuck ups *make her*
damaged goods?
Your mistakes simply *prove to her* what
she has tried to ignore.
It was your accomplishments that fucked her up.

**It was the way you said those words that
made her believe lies.**

It wasn't the way you constantly *buy two tickets*
to your rollercoaster relationship without
permission.
It was not the mistakes you regret
that made her **regret you**.
It was those *torturous good moments she*
believed.
Your attempt at goodness *robbed her off hers.*

Your attempts at true love showed her your
masking of fake.

Other side

The worst pain is loving someone who does not
love you. I mean, *or so they say.*
Of course, it's all a matter of perspective and
opinions. Pain is relative.
A stab here can hurt you perhaps more than it
would hurt me. Perhaps I have been stabbed there
before, you can't know,
that there is my point exactly.
Comparison over pain is foolish for there is no
way of truly knowing.
But have you ever been on the *other side of the
table?*
I guess these roots of pain only grow within
people like me, people who consider sides.
Selfless people who live life to be a
pleasurable remembrance.

**To be someone's memories of light
when in the dark days.**

If these roots *hold too little importance* and
refuse to grow within you, fix yourself.
Why have pain *that we can't share?*
Why watch one struggle when we could help?
Because if we are forced to live with it, *then
live with it we shall.*
Have you ever been on the other side of the
table?   *Because I have.*
Pain is something you *can't turn your back on.*
Pain *demands attention.*
You ever received so much and given so little?
Sometimes it isn't desire but the right thing.
Love for unexplained reasons, demands pain.
Have you ever been genuinely loved *by Someone
you can't love?*
Now that shit just shreds my heart to pieces.

Awaited Lesson

You asked to be taught *without pronouncing the words*.
Your experiences *begged for lessons*.
So, life brought *me to you*

You see?

I am your consequence.

You see?

I am your punishment.

real what becomes of her

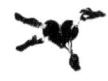 Trusting danger

Sweetie.

First man to get burned was because

he trusted the fire.

Love

This is how you make *them want you.*
This is how you make *them need you*
If that man can hook you on *a rollercoaster of*
expectations.
If he can do good *almost as often*
as he does bad.
If he tries at times as if everything
that happened *before doesn't count.*
How he builds another building *as apology to the*
other three he brought down.
He needs to feel *like danger and a strange*
feeling of home.
He needs to feel like excitement and *a*
Dangerously low amount of comfort.

He needs to be half of what he can be and a
whole product of what he desires.

She needs to *feel at home with his lies* so that
come time for dinner, she serves her *famous*
painkiller salad.

-Women really want this?
more than jewelry

120

Ignored strength

Why do I stay when I shouldn't?

What you don't seem to understand is that I will
take your *confused hate over your kempt leave of
absence.*
If the decision *was up to me,*
That's what I would choose *every time.*
That is why you need to understand that
it is you who needs to go.

Because I don't have the strength *in me* to fight
for me the way
I will fight for you.

Assertive acceleration.

She ate *all the red lights*.
She *never yielded or gave right of way*.
She hopped on that vehicle and pulled
out the driveway.
I stood in front.
Arms lay out, I was giving a choice;
Either stay or run me over on your way out.

She stepped on the gas like *it was her favorite
meal and she had been starving.*

Multiple choice

Empty yourself of all inside of you that
involves him.

The tears shed in his name.
The decision taken from his hate.
A hate that smelled a lot like love.

Because it just isn't fair, *to live for someone*
that refuses to live for you.
Foolish it is to crave his existence when yours
isn't even on his list of priorities.

He is wrong of course, but so are you

For wanting the wrong answer to a question
with so many right ones.

Bad person

I hate that your actions were reasonable.
I hate it because *the pain they left was not*.
I hate that you're a helping person.
I hate it because when I needed you,
you ran out of aid to give.
I hate that you are a good person, *I hate it*.

Because to my heart,
to my heart you don't feel like one.

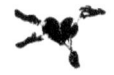

Played

She offered that *sweet pearl between her thighs*
Said is all boys want. Said 'at *this moment is*
all I want too'
So, I did, I accepted the offer and took every
ounce of pleasure that came with it.
Not because it was all I wanted nor because
it was all she wanted.

But because I had to show her that this
comfortable comfort between two connected souls
wasn't just physical.
That in order to truly fuck, *you must love.*
I had to show her what it felt like, *so I did.*

Now here I am holding a ring corresponding
to one of her fingers.

There she is, *not showing up.*

Dysfunctional heart

So, what if you remain *in my thoughts and desires?*
What am I to do to find love when my heart *cannot forget you?*

What am I to do to find happiness when my **heart does not wish for anything but you?**

What am I to do with *a dysfunctional heart?*
What am I to do with a heart that lives to die for you?

Conscious sin

I think you're *a disgrace.*
You're a *disgrace to somebody's life.*
You're a *disgrace to somebody's love.*
You're a disgrace to the return
policy of love.
To the *'giving amendment'* of life.
Your self-interests *aren't*
even beneficial to you.

They aren't beneficial to the flow of life.
So why practice useless tactics?

Why practice pain as a career?

It isn't because you cause it to somebody else
or because *you caused it to yourself.*
But *because you knew.*
You disrespected the laws of love, consciously.
So yeah, **I think *you're a disgrace to love.***
Like it says in the book of prophets.

'If anyone then, knows the good they ought to do
and doesn't do it,
it is a sin for them'

-This one isn't your mistake.
It's his

Wrong decider

Sometimes we mistake *bravery for cowardice*.
Because we intertwine the why's with the what's
and we assume *we just know*.
So, we call that man leaving a toxic love,
brave.
But he *was the toxic in his relationship*.
He was the black sheep in their commitment.
Yet, she sustained her life around such *idle
idea of love, against such lazy
representation of it*.
She gave herself to him, so if he leaves
he'd take her with him.

He would just leave the foundation of *all she
could have been*, to do a lot of homework on *the
subject of who she will be*.

Sometimes we *mistake bravery for cowardice*.
They called him brave for leaving.
But he shouldn't have been the one who left.

Naked representation

Skeletons are funny *don't you think?*
They can't smile, *can't frown*.
Emotion is something a skeleton
cannot reflect.
This is what you showed me.
You showed me the skeleton of your love. I need
skin for texture.

I need blood for proof.

A copy and paste of the basics.
A naked representation of *a clothed subject.*
The structure of what we *could have built.*
But how is a skeleton supposed *to live
without organs*?
How is it supposed to survive without the
covered strength your skin provides?
Your skeptical love could *not assure me enough.*
**Your skeptical love drowned in a puddle of
reliance.**

To add to the cause, *I don't think these bones
could float.*

The need to stop

I can only love you more than I love me
if you love me more than you love you.

Do I miss you more than *I miss me?*
I did my part, *you half-assed yours.*
But I did exactly what I was supposed to.

Do I miss you more *than I miss me?*
Because that is *exactly what I make it seem*
like.

Cruel joke

I miss you.

I miss being whole.

I miss so many things that *can never return.*

Life allows you to try samples when they are out of stock.

It *mocks your desires with false probability.*

A mockery to our hearts.

Now who are you to enforce *such a cruel joke?*

Plural pain

I have two cigarette *burns on the back of my
left hand.*
I do not know why they call it the back of the
hand *when it's what everyone sees.*
The palm should be the back, maybe that same
confusion is what confused me about *love's front
and back doors.*
I don't know whether *I came out of one to enter
another*, or *entered another to get out of one.*

**Doesn't matter, I still have two *cigarette burns*
on the back of my left hand.**

One *because I failed to feel* and the other
because I succeeded.
One smaller than the other because I wasn't
hurting enough at the time **to mask
the pain of the burn.**
Because *the hole in my chest* was not as big as
it was when *my skin put out that second
cigarette.* A pain I myself cause others *and
myself*, gets rewarded with physical pain, *to me
from me.*
It is stupid, it is inappropriate.
It isn't about the *enjoyment of inflicting
myself pain.*
But I guess pain told me I deserved it.
I deserve much *more of it.*
Doesn't change much.
I have two cigarette burns on the back of my
left hand.
I smoked those cigarettes *for clearance,*
they didn't give it to me.
**So, I extinguished the flame of my pain
with the skin of my hands.**
Just like you extinguished the flame of
our love with the skin of yours.

Glotoneria

You wanted *from me* a world that was *never
mine to give.*
I *became a thief* to *become a giver to you.*
I gave you something that was never mine to
begin with and you *could not
share your possessions.*
I didn't want those *to announce ownership*, but
to know if you'd sacrifice for me a fraction
 of what I would sacrifice for you.

**Because I needed to know that if we starve
tomorrow, your hand would be in the oven just
like mine was yesterday.**

I needed to know that you would also *leave a
piece of yourself* at love's doorstep.
Now I am making amends with the mistake I made
of *giving too much when you gave too little.*

Shoebox memories

So, I just remembered, I have your
memories *in my shoebox.*
Right, those memories aren't yours, *they're
ours.* I don't have them there because *I can't
let go of those moments* or because *I can't seem
to forget you.*
I don't wish to forget you actually.
*I have our memories boxed in because in that
moment I too was,* yet look at me smiling.
Look at me hugging a person I should be hating.
I was living in a jail cell of *pretty colors and
decorated bars.*
I was living in a prison of *all my desires.*
Eating enough of your attractions just to keep
me alive *when I should have been well fed.*
So, I just remembered I have our memories in my
shoebox inside my closet.
**I have not thrown them out yet because my
garbage has not stunk enough to deserve the
smell *of those rotten emotions.***
I have not burned them yet because fire
concludes everything it touches, so how can I
end something that barely begun?
Like justifying the reasoning behind your lies
simply because I moved on.
No, those boxed memories *shall stay there.*
When my desires disguise themselves as my
necessities again.
I'll open them.
I'll remember, *because a lesson this big cannot
be forgotten.*
So, they will remain in that box.
Compressed between those four corners, like I
once was.,
Folding the corners for comfort, begging to be
free.

Fire or not.

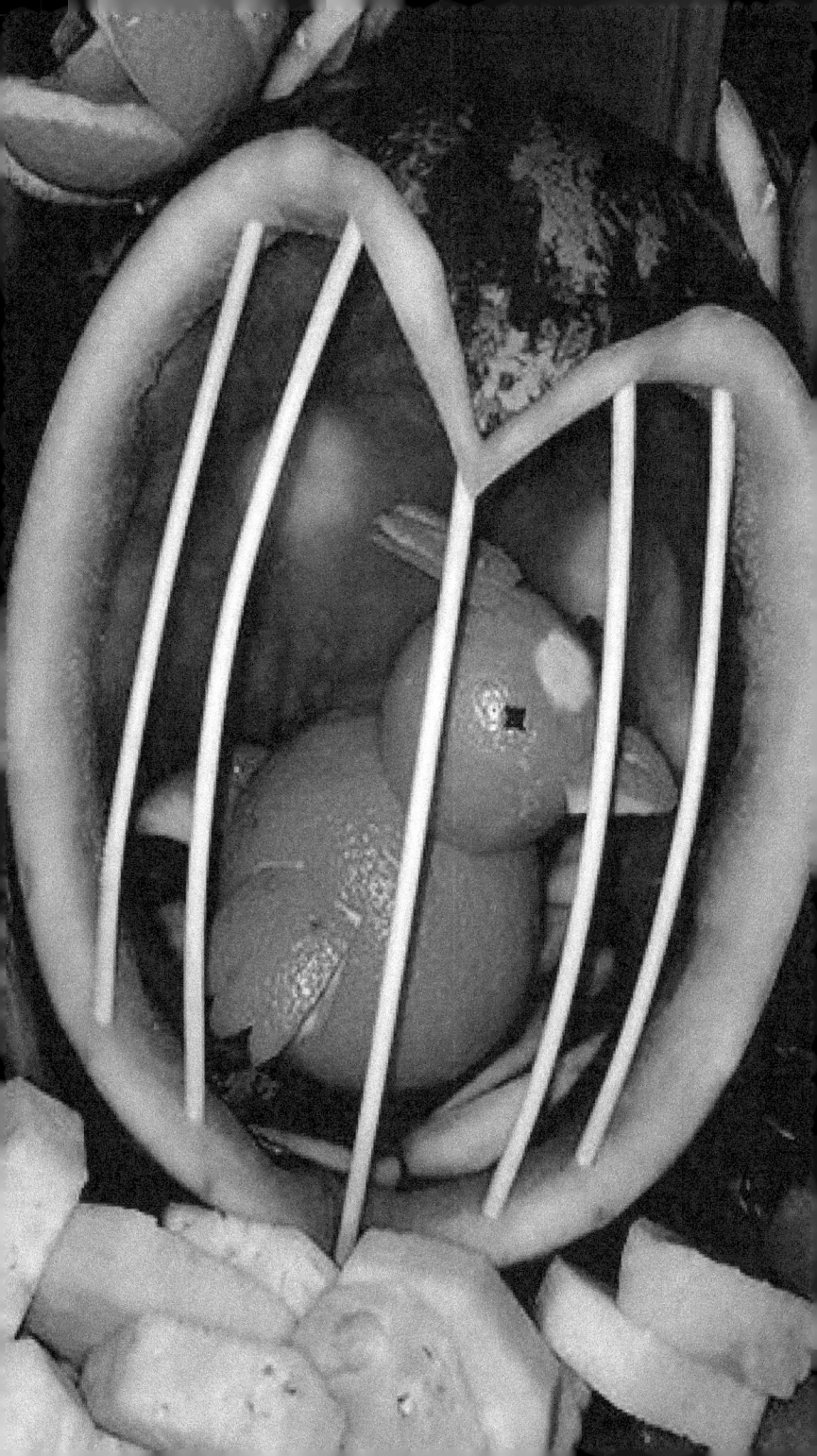

Lack of me

This one is for the almosts.
The ones that almost were *but never had a chance
to be*.
The ones with criminal lips *vandalizing*
another's.

This one is for *your heart*.

Remedy for the scars you never got, remedy for
the heartache we both saved *ourselves by
cracking our hearts*.
This one is for the possible futures, **the good,
the bad** and **the probable.**
This one is *for me.*
To hold me tight when I miss her in my life, to
choke me blue *when I disrespect her memory.*

This one is the cure for an aching heart.

To relieve *a passing feeling*.
To regret making a home for it.
This one is for your home *inside of me*.
For the dust on the kitchen counter.
For the rotten fruit on the dining table.
This one is for you,
so that you come back when you
feel the lack of me inside of you.

Chao's personal

...but I will still choose to lose myself *in the chaos* rather than agree to a peace that smells like temporary,
  that which is empty of adventure.

I would give myself to the chaos rather than stand by it.
Rather than *starve by it.*

I gifted myself to the chaos and all I got it was **a couple of bruises,**
some cuts and a big old heartbreak.

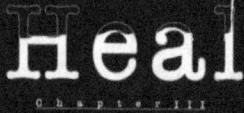

Heal

Chapter III

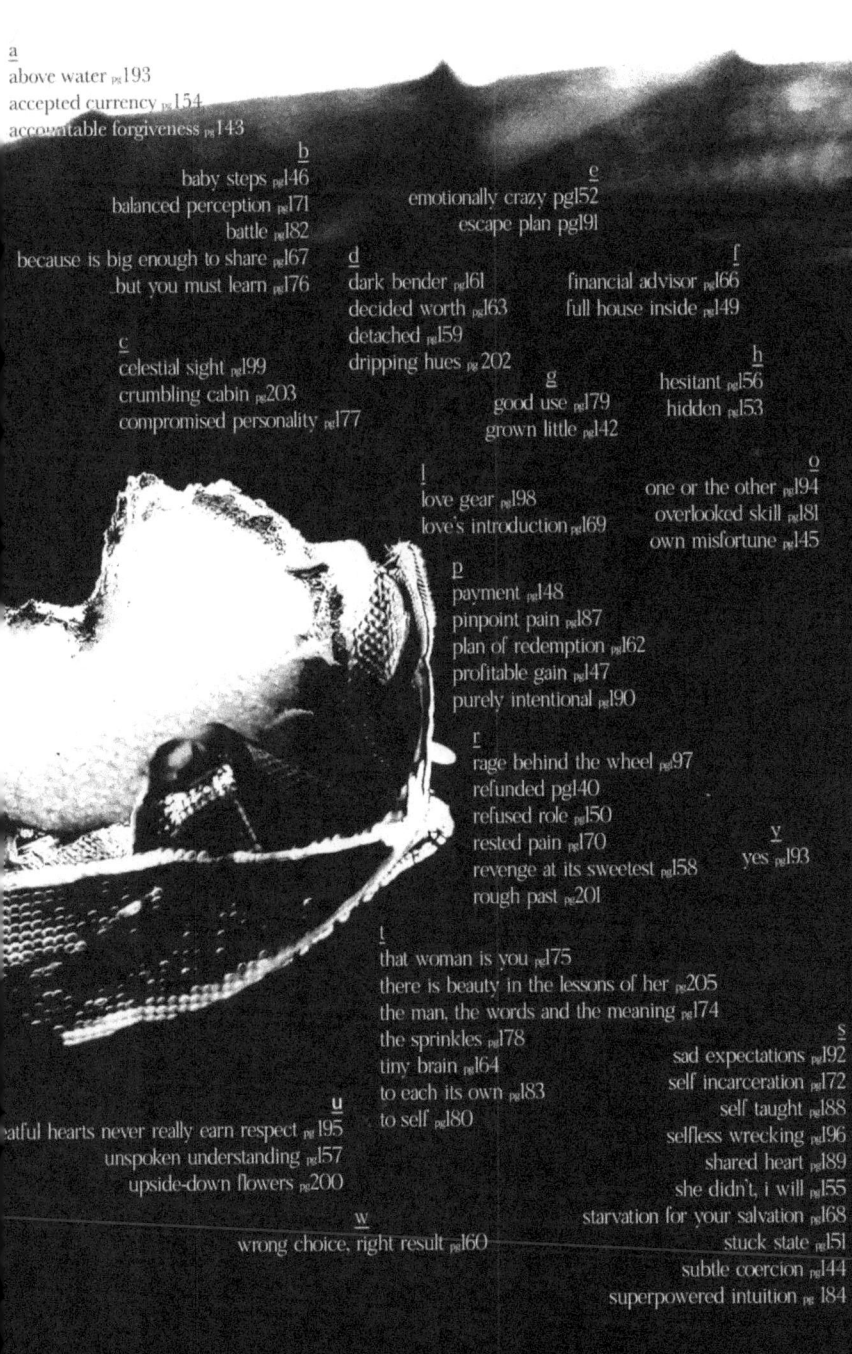

subtle coercio

Refunded

It's terrifying, *I know*.
To think that one day he *might wake up feeling differently*.
To think that one day he might not think about you *the way he does now*.
It's terrifying, I know.

But love does not cower away because of insecurities.

It does *not stop because of fear*.
Keep on loving and *keep on being loved* and if the day ever comes *where he does not want you*.
I think that's reason enough to not want him, *don't you think?*

After all, **love *is big on returns***

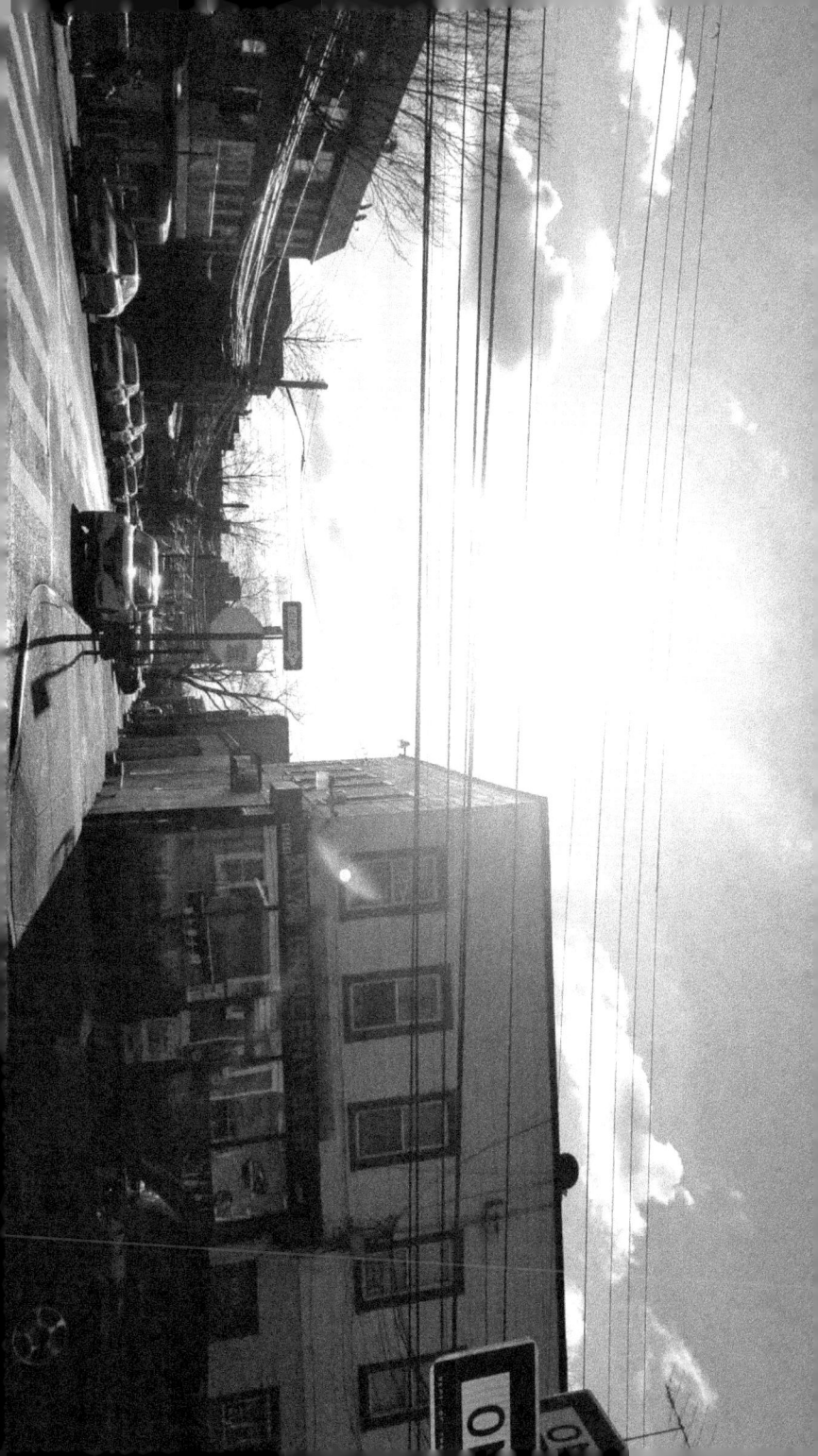

Grown Little

Baby girl you have to learn *to respect yourself*
These little boys won't.
That's when the men start appreciating you.

Wait for that.

Do not choose to *waste valuable time*
in these childish games.

Accountable forgiveness

It is hard to let go of people, especially when
the opposite was
your goal for a while.
Gets to the point where your love for him starts
making excuses for their actions.
Like we did as kids *to our mothers.*
Desperately trying to *instill belief.*
Minimizing the terrible damage they made because
holding accountability would mean letting go.

Hold them accountable *as you do yourself.*
Show them that *selfish decisions have selfish
consequences.*
Teach him what he never meant to teach you.
Because if laws are broken, does he think he is
above the law?
Is he above *you?*
If we ourselves pay for our actions
without break.
Then they should pay *for theirs.*

Let them dry up in *the desert of your
consequences.*

Subtle coercion

So, you hear his words *carefully when they sound too good to be true.*

You don't accuse.
You don't doubt the sincerity of his lies.
You don't align blame of subtle coercion.

You make sure his words **are** too good.
You make sure his words **are** true.

Own Misfortune

Take my hand, I *will come with you.*

I will come be alone with the company of only
you.
I will be lonely with you.
I will make sure **the darkness feels at ease**
with the misfortune of us.

Baby steps

...but if you fall in love with a man
without any.

Fall in love with love.
You must have a bond with love first; you must
be on first name basis with love.
Instagram pictures with *heartfelt*
captions and all.

Otherwise it will not introduce itself to him.

Profitable gain

Some people see nothing wrong with *giving too much* and *receiving too little*.
Just as long as they *receive something.*

They're desperate.

Those are the sellers you look for, to obtain profitable gain.
Because somewhere along the line, the ones giving too little will realize that they *will always receive.*
No matter how much they give.

Now, when you find a product cheaper than what you are used to paying *and just as good*, you are telling me you would not *invest in your savings?*

Payment

"...*but he loved me''* she *struggled to say* with
the chains of his commitment *around her
neck.*While patching up her scars.
Perhaps he did.

Perhaps he does.

That is the price we pay, for hurting the ones
who would never hurt us.
You shouldn't have to pay.
Victims don't pay; *victims get paid.*
Your payment is a fresher version of yourself,
one *you won't even recognize.*
One wearing freedom without embarrassment.
A clearer view of *who you wish to be.*
The price we pay for hurting those who would
never hurt us *is lingering love for them.*

You shouldn't *have to pay.*
You shouldn't have to *love the ones who hurt
you.*

Full house inside

I will tell you why *she didn't take*
your offer.
You kept offering her things *she already had.*
You offered her a half empty glass of water when
She legally owned oceans.
You offered her things that *did not interest her*
anymore. Things less than what she had.
You offered a tiny piece of your heart when *she*
has many.
You offered her a finger *when she*
needed a hand.

You offered her an umbrella when
she was the rain.

So how could she take you up on that offer?
A deal is done *when it is of convenience to all*
parties.
So how can she accept that offer, when she
already has everything *that suits her?*

You offered her an umbrella when
she was the rain.

Refused role

I am because of you.
I am in spite of you.
But I am not for you.

- not anymore anyway

stuck state

I have heard her say *'that is just the way I am'*
before.
I have heard her say that multiple times to
protect and excuse irrational behavior.
As if that is a valid excuse.
As if it is okay to do wrong simply because you
have always done wrong.

**I have heard her say *'that is just the way I am'*
more times than I have seen her care about who
she could be.**

She puts more effort into *complaining about the
things she doesn't like than into changing them.*
I have seen her protect her ignorance more than
I have seen *her embrace her potential.*
I have seen her *fail for a stationary answer.*
I have seen her lie to herself.
I have heard her say *'that is just the way I am'*
almost as many times as she sys 'it is what it
is' and to those *who don't know.*

It is not *'what it is'.*
It is *what you make it be,* and you are *who you
wish to be...*

Emotionally crazy

She said 'oh *I am crazy*'
So, *I believed her.*
So, *I left her.*

*Because crazy people don't know that they're
crazy, so why be*
with someone who wants to be?
If you want to be a writer, *you study the art in
the combination of words.*
If you wish to be a driver, you study the
art behind the wheel.
If you wish to be something, *you train to become
one.*

**So why be with someone who feels
the need to prove insanity?**

Just why?
When *sanity brings about much*
more pleasure and enjoyment.
She said *she was crazy.*
And she was.
But that is **because she wanted to be.**

I have never met a person with such
low emotional intelligence.

Hidden

So, what if you show me your *cracked body* and I
happen to have an attraction *towards things that
aren't perfect?*
So, what if you show me your thoughts and I
happen to have **a fetish for wild ones?**
So, what if you *undress and show me your
skeletons* and I just went ahead
and did the same?

Have you thought of *any of those possibilities
before lying?*

Accepted Currency

So, *if I help you with the search* I have only
but one wish from you.

That is absolute safety for my heart.

If you can't find these instructions marked on
any of the days of your agenda.
I apologize, you're looking for the wrong thing
in the right place.

She didn't, I will

How twisted is that?
We learn to love ourselves from *the people who failed to.*

Hesitant

If you hesitate on the choice of me.
Don't *choose me.*

I never considered *for a millisecond the*
possibility of not choosing you.

I need that.

Unspoken understanding

Since they need words *for clarification*.
Clarify.
Since they need clarification *for understanding*.
Explain.

But her heart is a commitment *fueled by*
good intentions.
Her heart is an oath *of extreme caution.*
She shouldn't have to tell you *for*
you to know.

They have to understand without explanation *the*
way I did -the protection of your heart is an
unspoken understanding.

Revenge at its sweetest

If *the magnitude of your actions* is something
you decide *not to see.*
If the blood is something you refuse *to wash off*
your hands.

You must know.

Acting like it isn't a car in front of you *does*
not make it a bicycle.
Blinding your *hearts needs* with your desires
does not justify the *disrespect shown to love.*
How can you ever expect it to respect you when
those plans **were far too many days ahead**
on your agenda?
How can you claim what you deserve when that *is*
exactly what you have provided yourself?
If you ever decide *you do* want better.
If you stop procrastinating **in the**
affairs of the heart.
Simply *be better.*
Patience has run its course, tolerance its
termination.
You must know.
It *hurts you now* more *than it hurts me*, because
your actions were *completely*
uncalled for.

Mine, **revenge.**

Detached

Go deep *within yourself.*
Find the seeds he planted,
even if they sprouted.
Find *the parts of him* that fell on you.
The ones that found a home *on*
the grounds of you.

The ones that feeds on you to grow on you.

Find it.
Have your moment with it, *then free it.*
That is the only way to *leave him*

Wrong choice, right result

I can cherish your memory.
I could.
The same way I know *you cherish mine.*
But why would I cherish the memory of a person
who could not *cherish the reality of me*?
A person who has made me their biggest regret
when I should be *their biggest accomplishment.*
A man whose actions *became the death of him.*
A man who decided to walk on fire, **barefoot.**
A man who ran away at *the glimpse*
of his toes burning.

Why would I cherish who continuously *antagonized*
my presence?

I can't deny the satisfaction
of those moments.
But I cannot accept the catastrophic weight
of his acts of heroism.

Because the reality of me *is to be cherished.*
The reality of me is to be embraced.

Dark bender

They *threw her* in the *den of darkness.*

She vanished.

She came back with the realization that *she only*
needed to control her darkness,
 then the rest would follow.

She came back *controlling her shadow*,
no matter where the sun shone.

Plan of redemption

Emerge whole.

Destroy those *who failed* to complete you
by completing yourself.

Decided worth

My worth comes *in droplets of efforts*.
In willing scarification.
My worth comes *in bundles of clear intent*.
In *packs of desire.*
My worth comes in many shape and forms,
none hard *but all difficult.*

My worth comes in very specific ways
**to show that you don't only *want to* win my
heart, but you *need to*.**

My worth comes in all these forms because *I need
to know you know* before
I decide that I do.

Tiny brain

Intuition is like a tiny human
that lives inside of us. It always has urges and
sometimes-unimportant demands.
But at this point, it's been there for so long,
you kind of forget about it.

You know we never really appreciate presence
as much as we do departure.

We never really appreciate things that are there
as much
 as things we want there.
Because I guess in a way to balance this tiny
human, we also *have tendencies of*
self-destruction.

Because he's right and *we're always wrong.*

This tiny human lives in my head, so if I were
to write a report on him and his location was
the subject.
It would be inside of me, *right?*
The disrespect I showed him, was disrespect
shown to me, *because he is me.*

How can I ever say I don't know what it is I
need to do, when I was *telling myself what was*
right, from the very start?

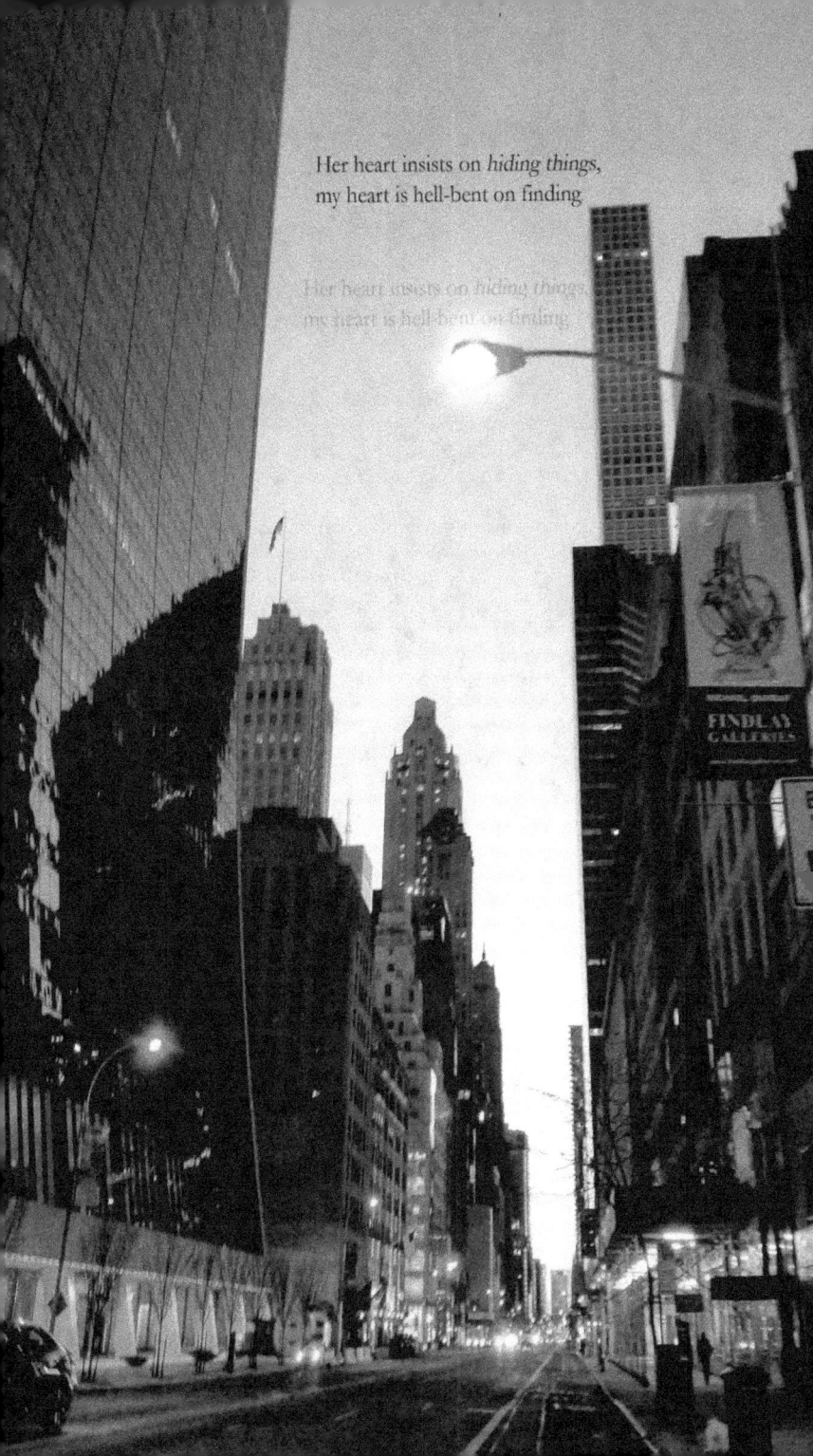

Her heart insists on *hiding things*,
my heart is hell-bent on finding

Financial advisor

Just because you can't find the right buyer
doesn't mean *the price of*
your product suffers.
Price only diminishes when the seller
is desperate.
Just because no one seems to have enough doesn't
mean your worth is on clearance.

You started leasing your skin to
the ones who could not buy it
You started renting your heart to
the ones who could not buy it.

You financed yourself to the ones *with various*
expenses, **just to keep the dust**
off your surface.
Hoping that every month *their payments add up.*

They almost never do.

Renting your skin and financing your heart, *I am*
thinking I should manage your properties.

I am waiting here for you to make me
your financial advisor.

Because is big enough to share

Sipping my drink, *evaluating your equations*.
You forget to show the work that was demanded,
so points off.

Don't mind me, just checking if you qualify *to
own even a small portion of my heart.*

Starvation for your salvation

He expects *the benefits of your body* and
refuses the benefits of your soul

wow

**That is a man who was never taught
the extravagant flavor of growth.**

*The warm feeling of desire toward changing your
ways to show off to one*
 who will always comply.
Like we're little kids again playing and running
around at *the expense of our growth.*

If the benefits of your body are the *only
privileges he seems to want.*

Let that man starve.

Love's introduction

There is one simple fact *reassuring my peace when I see* the new men in your life.

That is no matter *who you meet,* no matter *who you fuck.* **You met love because of me**

Rested pain

You need to come with me *where it's safe.*
You must hold my hand *to disperse the shadows.*
You must *find place* in this corner of life,
you must learn comfort.
You must learn to trust.
But you need to come with me *where it's safe.*
Come, let's put this pain to rest.

Balanced perception

We whisper our emotions so that any
distracted ears *can't hear.*
We whisper our emotions so that we can
get a medal for participating.
Because if we whisper them instead of keeping
them in, at least *we did our job.*
Because if they didn't hear me,
then **it was them *who didn't do theirs*.**
So I did *my part.*

I whispered my emotions for a *healthier mind.*
For a balanced perception.
I whispered,

 But I forgot *how hard* my eyes could shout.

Self-incarceration

Who were you when *I had not appreciated* the
pleasure of being there?
Who were you *before him?*
Who were you during him?
Curiosity has been the death of many, I'll take
death *at the cost of meeting you.*
The you, *you*.
To the extreme of getting to know *those troubles*
that made your skin adapt.
Who were you *when you were with him?*
Why did **she** cause you to change?

What was it that she did that made you
hate her?

What was it that she said that *turned you
against yourself?*
What was it that she *accused you* of doing?
Because *whatever it was*
It is not worth this trial you put yourself
through. This self-incarceration is not justice
to your crimes.

Crimes of morality.
Like stealing food for the homeless.

Who were you *before him?*
Because whoever *she was*. **Give her space to
breathe**
.
You need to *cut her some slack.*

Whatever her mouth spoke, she became

The words, the man and the meaning

I just want her to get lost in the words and
their meanings...

maybe *then she'll find me.*

Hard to find him who *hides from himself.*

But who knows,
  maybe my next metaphor will do the trick

That woman is you

I hope one day you seduce the woman who stares
back at you *in the mirror.*

Have your way with her.

She deserves *every bit of you.*

..but you must learn

Why would I *try to change her* if she's who
I fell in love with?
Why *would I fall in love with somebody*
I want to change?
I am not here to be *trial* and *error*.
I'm not here to shape and nurture you so that
the next can enjoy you.
If you can't *understand your own need* of change
and development,
then *it must be life the one to teach you.*

Not me.

Compromised personality

Compromise your personality only for the sake of
teaching necessary lessons.
You should *do you* but while that someone is
around, do who *you have to,* to teach them *what
they need to learn*
When they leave your sight, don't
confuse *your two personas.*
*Choose one as primary and foundation of the
other.*
It is not double face at all,
just desperate measures.
Some don't learn as fast as they should,
some drop the knowledge they try to grasp.

Trust me a *compromised personality* would drive
an accustomed man insane.

Use that instead.

The sprinkles

That space reserved, the one you make sure to
keep *empty of you because you are waiting for it*
to be full of him.
It's a waste of space.
That destructive desire,
a waste of opportunity.
Because **we look for** *things we want*
and **wait for** *things we need.*
Want something better.

Have standards in the appearances of hearts.
Stop wasting that space and *give it some use.*

Fill it up with you and *when* you find him,
let him be the sprinkles.

Good use

May these words become of use to you and
your development.

To self

No matter how much you love him.
It is still not enough to excuse *being
with him.*
No matter *how much* you love him.

You should love you more.

Overlooked skill

Once you became mine you waved your right to
your *hearts personal integrity and I could not
even keep my own*
You trusted me to drive stick when I never
mastered the maneuvering behind the
automatic wheel.

This isn't a transfer of guilt.

This is recognition of blame *from both sides*.

Battle

Fight for me when you think
I will change my mind.
Fight for me when you *think I won't.*

I just **need to see you fighting.**

I can't give my heart to one who just roams the
place when *others have killed for it.*
Their attempts *demand respect* and even though
they're the past ones, the lessons are *still
here* in the present.

Fight for me.
Make the battle for my heart *the
only priority of yours.*

Maybe **then it falls.**

To each its own

Oh, *this is it?*
This is how *you intend to* move on?
I guess I can't do anything but *accept what I*
once criticized.
I guess I *can't do much* but accept what
I just now came to learn.
But of course.

However the pain lessens.

Super powered intuition

If *you were to know your worth*, would you act
according to that knowledge?

Will it rain pigs?

Will it cause the ground to spit *rain up to the
sky?*

Tell me, would it light this world on fire
if you acted like you should?
Because you reject *to acknowledge your worth*
as if it disgusted you.
As if this 'better' version of you *masks* a bad
one.

Would it rain from the ground up if you decided
to act accordingly?

**Because if all it does is *change your
circumstances*, *which is exactly what you need
changing*,** why the hell deny yourself of
salvation?

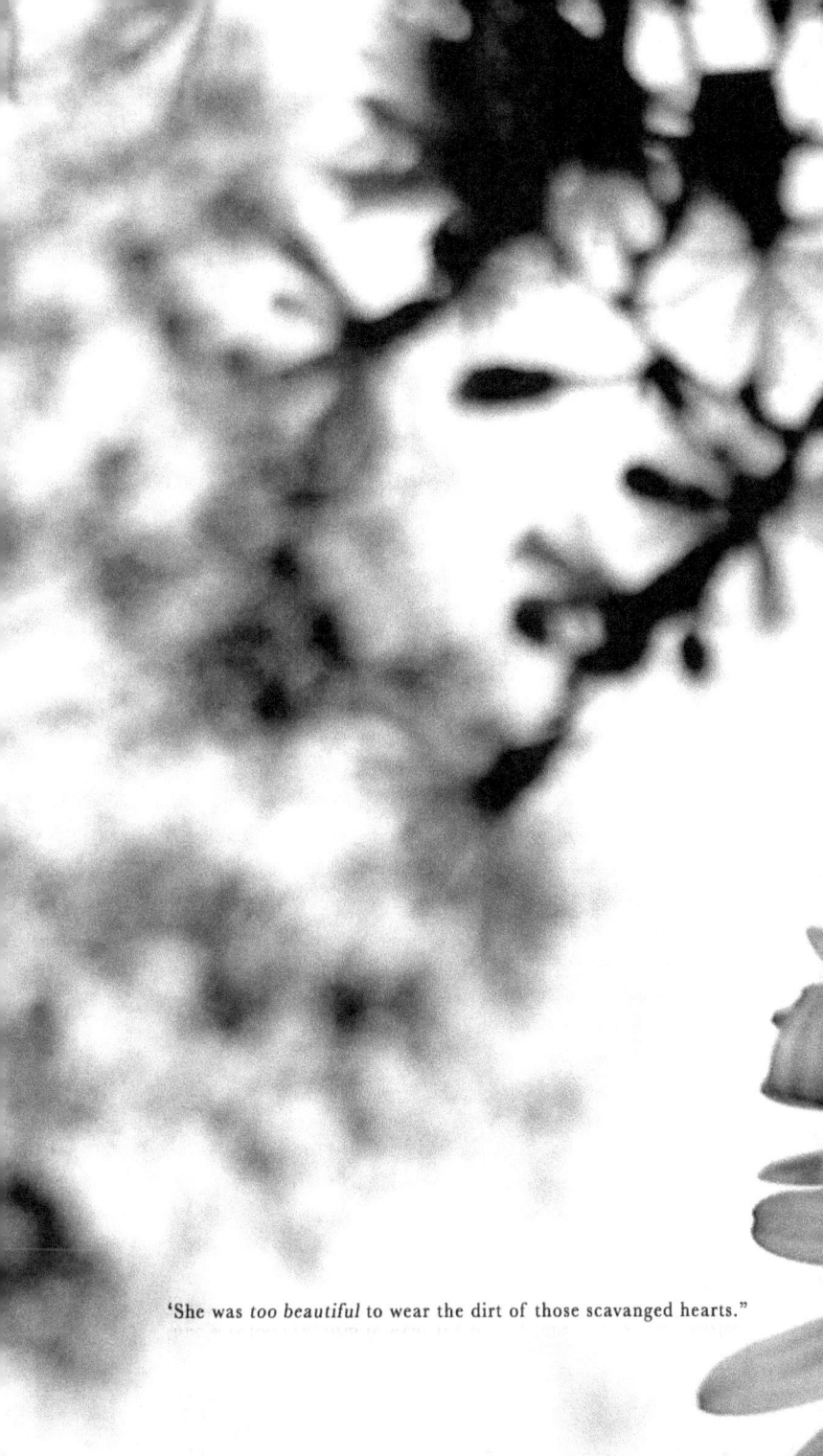

'She was *too beautiful* to wear the dirt of those scavanged hearts."

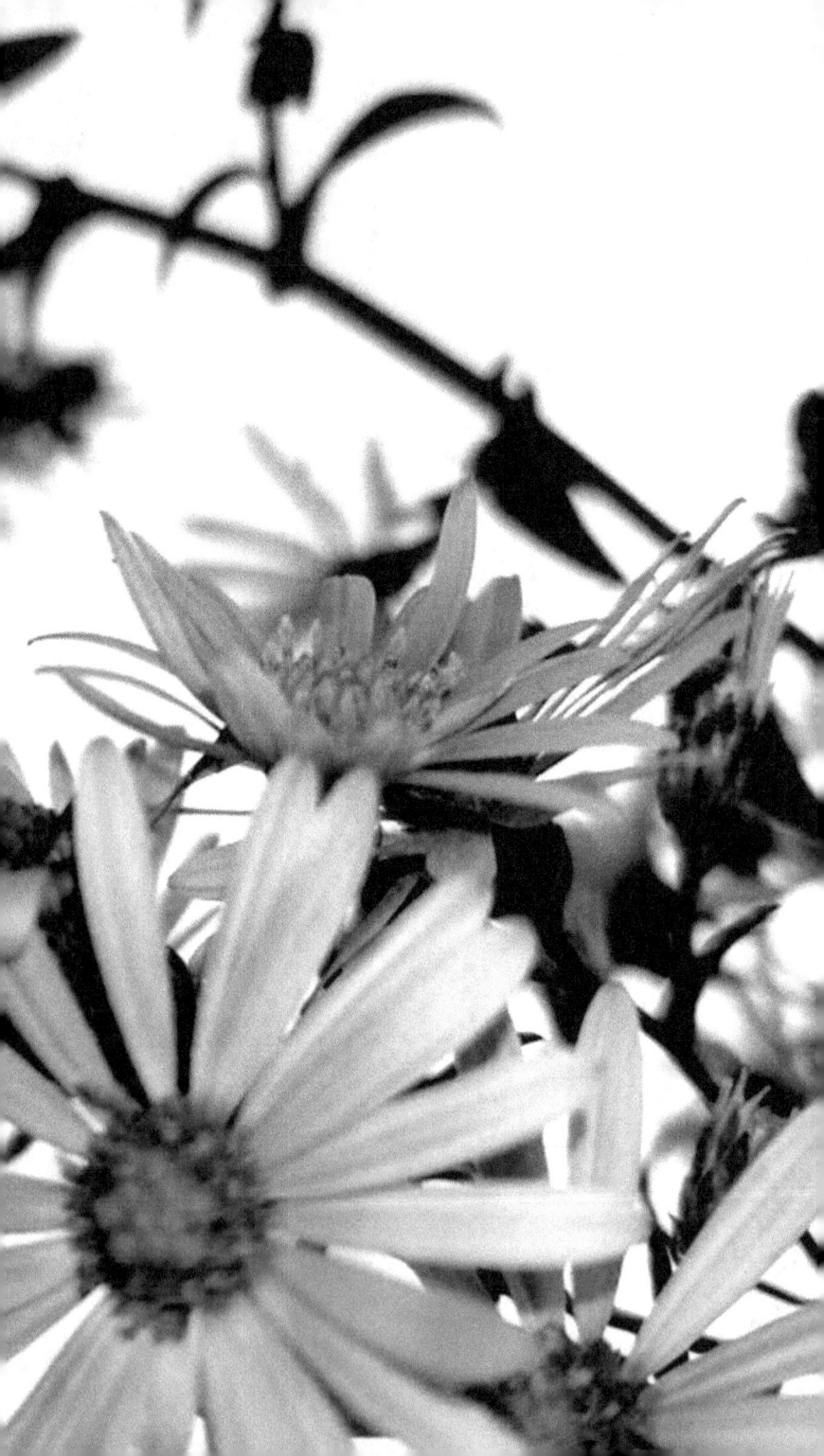

Pinpoint pain

Sometimes I do not know *what it is* I feel.
I think that's *perfectly okay.*
Because a heart *this big* with emotions *this deep*
does not always need *a specific* reason to break.
Life is reason enough.
In a world like this with *unfairness this deep,*
my tears do not need a specific *reason to fall.*
When you fill a cup with water and keep pouring,
the *water spills.*
What are emotions if not *an addition to pain?*
What are emotions if not an *addition to joy?*
Feeling *is the only thing we know* how to do.
It is the only thing we do *without error.*
So please, **when I can't pinpoint the**
 reason for my sorrow.
Asking me will just *remind me of that.*
How about instead you *do what I do and*
feel it with me?

Self taught

How am I supposed to *get to know you* when you
rejected *your own formal introduction to
yourself?*

Shared heart

If you *don't feel it.*
Don't *pretend to.*
Don't act as if your confusion somehow has a
permission slip to the hallways *of my life.*
I made those
Like so many times you said your feelings had
changed, *follow them.*
Take them with you on your way out.
But leave *and also walk away;* I don't need a
lingering scent of you *around my food.*

This is the place I eat.
This is the place I rest.

If you don't like *the comforts of it,*
why stay?
If you can't find a place to lay down your life
while I am here *waiting for you to,*
simply go elsewhere.
Your confusion *fails to spare me pain.*
Your confusion works for you, *not for me.*
If you *don't feel it.*
Don't *pretend to.*
Don't act as if your confusion is anything
shorter than *a paper-thin heart*
choosing to be shared rather than cherished.

Purely intentional

The only way to know if someone truly deserves
you. Is only *if they earn you.*
I am not talking about flowers and pretty words,
which could come from anyone.
But you must see their desire
to **protect your heart.**
You must feel the passion *in their caressing.*
The hope in their kisses.
You must be able to see and feel
their desires *for you.*
The way they change their energies so that
 it can correlate with yours.
You must *be able to see.*
When a man deserves you,
not seeing it *is purely intentional.*
Just like loving.
You *just know.*
So, if you're sitting somewhere reading this
thinking about someone.
If you can't measure their value to
the essence of you.

Not seeing that *would also be purely
intentional.*

Escape plan

When you finally realize *the mistake, it was for*
you; and the *blessing it was for me.*
When you finally start to notice *the lack of me*
inside of you and decide to *come for me.*
Know that *I will put some distance between us.*
I will fight love and **I will find hobbies**
to keep my heart busy.
Everything to extend that *imaginary distance*
between our hearts.

Funny, *isn't it?*

The fact that actions *have consequences.*
The reality that you *never took a second to*
consider me because you were satisfied.
Because you were well fed.
Funny how I used to *run after you.*
Now when you decide to run after me.

It will be me *running away from you.*

Sad expectations

Any one of your *poor attempts at replenishing*
your value ends up taking
more and more *from it.*
Your value decreases and I cannot think of any
other reason as to **why my heart is hurting.**
The stupid *conscious mistakes* have not only
crippled you.
It has me gasping; your mistakes
crack both our hearts.
You see, I see you *as a queen* while you
treat yourself *like a peasant*
by treating yourself to peasants.
Must adjust my expectations to
 your *low aspirations*
To your *poor attempts at feeling.*
My heart will keep reminding me of your
potential value.
Your actions will *keep reminding me* that
bettering yourself is not in your *to-do list.*
When you're old and gray or maybe just when I *am*
not there anymore to tell you these things.
You'll know.
You'll *thank me.*
For now I'll remain as your
annoying big brother.

For you, **I'll take the hatred.**

yes

if he put *no effort* in **keeping you**.
Put *no effort into making him stay.*

Above water

You *suffocated me under the* pressure
of your expectations only to find out
I can breathe under pressure.
You tried to drown me in the oceans of your
ways only to find out
I am a marvelous swimmer.
You tried to burn me with *the aftertaste of
your voice,* only to find out that
I can breathe the fire.

Forgetting that I am the fire.

You did everything in your power to make me
wonder if you wanted me.
To spend *the rest of my life fighting*
for a spot in you.
But *you forgot,*
    I can breathe just fine without you

*Ungrateful hearts never
really earn respect*

A few mistakes ago, I would have *made that
decision.*

Now countless of mistakes later...

No thank you, I will not give myself to
those **who never taught themselves**

to say thank you.

Selfless wrecking

I've got no time or reason *to reminisce*.

You see your memories and the emotions *I felt for you* have fallen through the *hole you left in my chest*.

Nothing ever comes back from there.

So, I apologize; you *were collateral* damage to the *destruction you left behind*.

Rage behind the wheel

Those *ugly words and thoughts* that escape
your mouth, squeezing for space *in your
head*, squeezing *between your teeth*.
Those lies you say to *the person that
is true to you,* due to anger.
Even though those words are to *be expected*.
The ones who *mean something* with their voice
and intentions.

Those people are to be respected.

Don't let anger get in the way of that,
nothing good ever came of it.

Love gear

Your love *for you* has to be *so strong* that
it *wears itself on the surface of your
being.* That it disguises itself with
helpful rejections.
That it disguises itself with *selfish words
for the good of your integrity.*

Your love *for you* has to be so strong that
it itself, *rejects any possible attraction
to* somebody, anybody who
Won't love you like you love you.

Celestial sight

Do you not understand that you are *a celestial sight?*
Heavens in pure flesh.
The embodiment of *all that is good* in this world. You are the heart of this world, I promise you, it would look different *without the magnetic attraction of your being.*

You are living proof of true love.

You are *a consequence* and a *blessing* all wrapped in the same gift.
You are all of this and yet
you think you need him.

If that isn't the perfect example of foolishness
I honestly do not know what is.

Upside down flowers

My mistakes bleed *all over my heart*.
My heart never dries so the blood **thickens**,
sticking to my surface.

Becoming part of my becoming.

The lessons I learned from you will be the
principles I follow *to stay away from you.*
My heart may not be in the best condition *it
could be.* Happiness may have taken a break
from my door.
Sorrow may have become a close friend.
But if I turn my back on these principles,
then I wouldn't have any.
If I turn my back on the principles *that
helped me rise above*, then *I drown right
there below you*.

I have never been one to *reject the sun* but
its absence **sometimes *comforts my soul*.**
I have never been one to *reject happiness*
but ***I sometimes welcome the cold***
.
That is because of that persistent truth
that feeds itself in this reality.

In sadness, we grow.

Rough past

Her lips were as *anesthetizing*
as lips could be.
Her heart was *as tender* as a heart
understood its need to be.

Dripping hues

...you're all that is left *you know.*
From **the love, the hues** and **the colors**.

Only you remained.

God made you *then hesitated to make anyone else.*
You shine brighter than all
these bullshit lies.

Love like love is proud to be you.

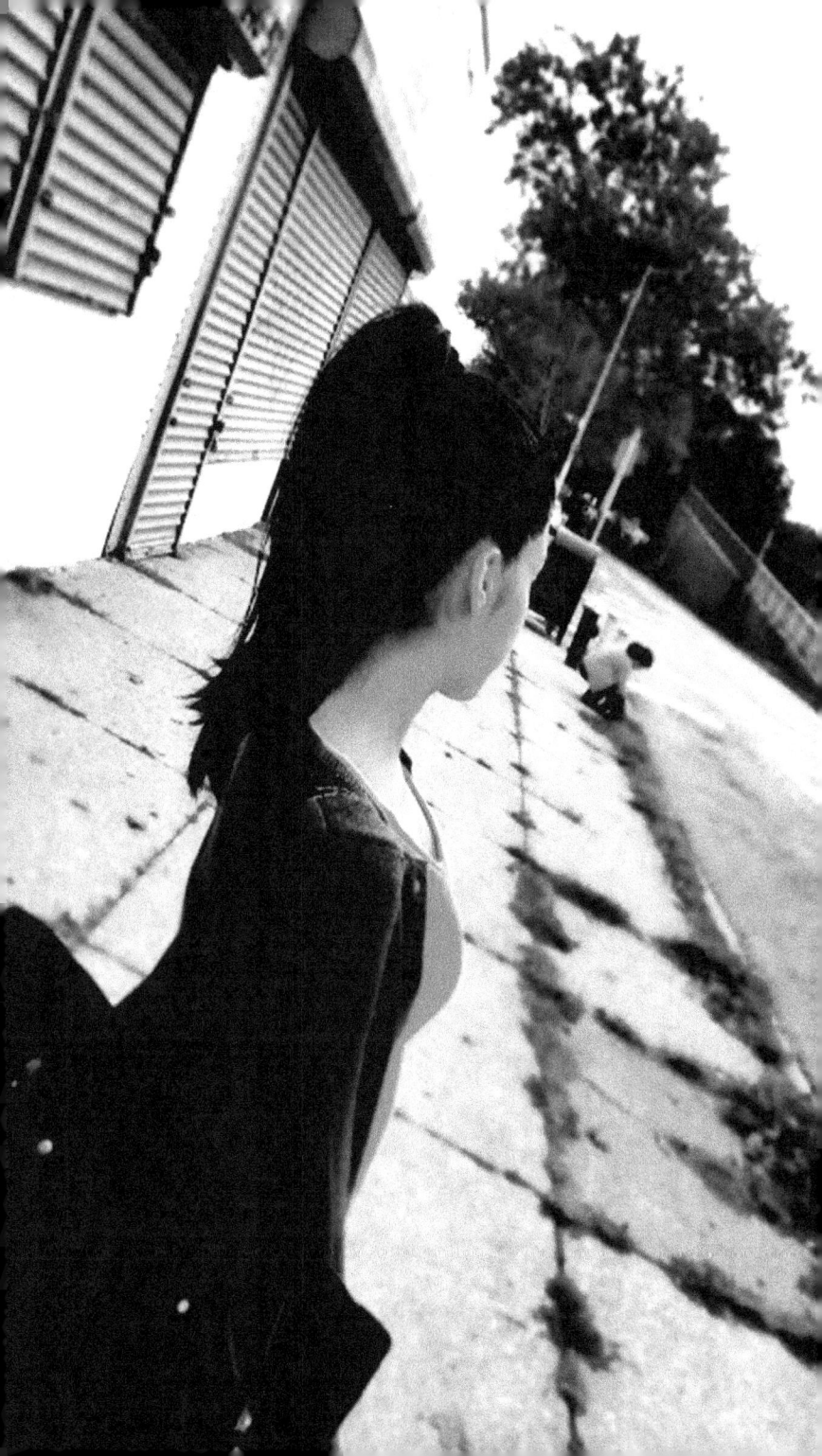

Crumbling cabin

Lock it.
If the doors aren't locked, *any wanderers*
can come in.
Anybody looking for shelter will find it
inside.
Lock the door tight with that combination
lock you were gifted with.
When a soul **knowing the combination of love**
opens it.
That is when you know they were meant to
walk in.
To find shelter in you.
That is when you open those doors,
but for the time being, *close them.*

Lock it.

Because any wanderer that *may come in will*
not respect the organized order
of your furniture.
The wont even respect the sheets you use to
cover your bed.

Muddy shoes as pajamas.

They'll leave a **crumbling cabin to avoid**
fixing it.
All because *you forgot to put that*
combination lock.
A price *too high* to pay *for*
an honest mistake.

This was '...**the mistakes of her**'

I could write an entirely different project
and still use the chapters.

Fall *again*.
Break *again*
Heal *again*.

Why tell you more about a cycle *you've
always lived?*
Why say *more words* when I've written dozens
of poems to try and facilitate what it is *I
am trying to say.*?

There were memories *I had to relieve* to
write down these words.
Memories that needed *closure from me,*
so they thank you.
I thank you.
I hope these words found a way
into your head.
I hope they softened the hardest parts
of your heart.

 I hope you never forget
how beautiful it is to be you.

For excerpts and updates on my oncoming books.

Instagram/ @thrives_on_falsehood @defied.perspective

I want to thank my friend; Gabriel Chacon Ruiz for that beautiful cover. May your hands continue to create those things appealing to the heart.

How beautiful is it to see
veterans of love?
To see her *broken in all her glory.*
To see the hurt for what it reveals and not
what *it pokes.* (wounds)
The mistakes of her was written because I
felt we see our mistakes as cause and *not as
effect.* Because in a puddle of unresolved
mistakes
many drown.

We've forgotten to respect **our failures.**
We've forgotten to respect our pain.
We've forgotten about our **commute to change,**
our commute to a better living.

We've forgotten to take a closer look
at *our mistakes.*
To study them and not just *regret them.*
To love them and not just their pleasure.
Maybe I am *oversimplifying the importance*
of our mistakes.
Ever got beaten down *by an old mistake
acting* as a future one?
Ever been held hostage by your shame?
Mistakes are ugly, deformed and unstable.
We'll use them as bait to attract the
darkness, and for once, **to kill it.**
So *hey.* I hope today has been sweeter than
the days before. I hope today you
experienced *something that felt like living.*
Shine brighter than *you did yesterday.* Love
like your hearts never *known heartache.*
Learn from the mistakes, *squeeze them.*
Extract light from the shadows, *disperse the
bad.*
Love you like you love them and
I promise you.

Your world will look like it used to.

There is beauty in the Lessons of her

Beauty is *reason to fall in love*.

Beauty *is peace* before the calm.

Beauty *are her lessons*.

Beauty *what she felt* from her mistakes.

Beauty is *a chance to win* love's war.

There is beauty in the mistakes of her

Like it or not.

By: Roberto Rodriguez

She has got ways of loving that love had no
business teaching.

It wasn't love *that taught her* to
love that way.

Then what did?

...the mistakes of her

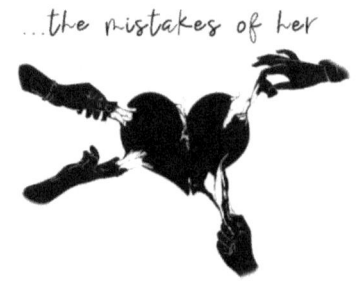